Navigating the New Normal

Navigating the New Normal

How New & Small Companies Can Succeed Despite Economic Uncertainty

Rodd Mann

BEP

BUSINESS EXPERT PRESS

Leader in applied, concise business books

Navigating the New Normal:
How New & Small Companies Can Succeed Despite Economic Uncertainty

First published in 2021 by
Business Expert Press, LLC
222 East 46th Street, New York, NY 10017
www.businessexpertpress.com

ISBN-13: 978-1-63742-020-1 (paperback)
ISBN-13: 978-1-63742-021-8 (e-book)

Business Expert Press Entrepreneurship and Small Business Management Collection

Collection ISSN: 1946-5653 (print)
Collection ISSN: 1946-5661 (electronic)

First edition: 2021

10 9 8 7 6 5 4 3 2 1

Description

No one will forget the year 2020.

The year that a pandemic shut down social, work, and public contact.

There are two particular changes that have had a pronounced effect on business and finance, which this book will provide the guidance currently lacking in traditional business school texts.

The first is the change from commuting to work to sheltering-in-place, with students and professionals on videoconferencing apps such as Zoom. Likely a lasting change, we can expect many office spaces will remain empty and many businesses will stick with the new work-from-home change.

The second change is that the younger generation is the first to suffer a setback in terms of the standard of living compared to their parents. Not only do more than half of Americans have less than $1,000 in savings, but they eschew traditional corporate cubicles, preferring instead to juggle multiple and new 'hustles and side gigs.'

This book is primarily focused on the post-pandemic Gen Z and Millennial business opportunities, most of which didn't even exist a generation ago.

Keywords

small business; economic uncertainty; pandemic; virus; COVID-19; vaccine; business owners; MBA students business planning; Gen Z; Millennials; financial management; corporate investing; investing; forecasting; finance; competitive advantage; competition; gig economy; side hustle; corporate social responsibility; Internet; government assistance; cash flow; raising capital; central banks; new paradigm; business risks; revenue growth; cost; profitability; vision; strategy; forecasting; cryptocurrencies; SWOT; outsourcing; regulatory environment; suppliers; employees; business metrics; cash flow; investment; flexible budgeting; business growth

Contents

CHAPTER 1

Basics and Some Online Business Ideas

Vision→Strategy→Tactics→Business Plan→Execution

Figure 1.1 Vision

We first identify the business we are planning to pursue or already find ourselves in today. Each type of business has common attributes, goals, and objectives, and their own unique characteristics that require good understanding and a strategy to optimize those characteristics and pursue the goals and objectives that have been set for the business. The broadest of these are manufacturing versus service businesses, with the primary difference that a manufacturing business sells a physical product whereas a service business sells a service. For instance, a hand sanitizer company is a manufacturing business. In contrast, a service business could be an accounting or a legal firm, or a mobile service that provides hand sanitizers at checkout registers of stores.

What constitutes a comprehensive vision? It includes the kind or type of business, comprehending the size and scope initially, intermediate-term, and long term. The vision lends itself to goal setting and objective seeking. It cannot be too pie-in-sky or when the time comes to operationalize your vision, you just may find the entire dream was just that—only a dream. The vision sets the company direction and has enough heft to make the development of a cohesive strategy an obvious and logical next action item.

Don't confuse your vision with a mission statement. They are different. A mission statement is a position you take for the stakeholders, for example, employees, stockholders, and customers to read in order to learn more about the nature of the business. A vision statement declares intentions of direction, where the company is headed, while a mission statement declares where the company is today.

We want to start a business and we already have the first step from which to take the sequence of steps needed to be successful. The first step is our *vision*. You foresee already what your business will be doing. You have thought about it, dreamed of it, and you now have in your mind's eye the mental picture of your very own business, up and running the way you would like to run it, and you are the boss. But have you asked yourself, what makes you and your vision uniquely qualified to take your product to market? Have you considered whether your business product line is too narrow or perhaps too broad? A Goldilocks approach to optimize the business offering could be stated in simple terms that what customers are expecting is what they will be getting. Too narrow and potential customers are going to find your competitor offering with more choices, variations and related accessories, and services. Too broad and you will find yourself competing with Amazon, a financial death wish.

Passion begets creativity and in turn innovation. Is your product truly innovative? If not, perhaps it is just a better, or cheaper, or faster, or functionally superior competing product. Not every business idea has to qualify for disruptive innovation that you might find at Apple or Tesla. Once you have settled the vision-related questions, it is time to move on to your strategy. Now, we turn to the next step in the development of our business plan.

Vision→Strategy→Tactics→Business Plan→Execution

Business strategy is the company plan aimed at achieving its vision. It goes further than the vision, prioritizing objectives, identifying the firm's competitive edge, and identifying how to optimize the financial results of the business.

The choice of the objectives is the centerpiece of the strategy, but a thoughtful and thorough approach also describes in concrete terms just how the company plans to meet each of these objectives. Practically speaking, the strategy illuminates how the business will differentiate itself from its competitors, how it will generate revenue, and what can be expected in gross margins and profitability from the revenue.

Strategies must honestly describe the company's strengths and weaknesses, along with its opportunities and threats.

Strategy begins with a list of primary milestones to pursue. The milestones must be mapped, noting those that must be sequential, versus those that can be accomplished in parallel, all dependent upon time and

	STRENGTHS	WEAKNESSES
INTERNAL	What do you do well? What resources do you have? What advantages do you have over your competition? What is your USP? People, property, process, products	What could you improve? What should you avoid? Limited resources Lack of access to skills or technology Poor location
	OPPORTUNITIES	THREATS
EXTERNAL	What opportunities exist in your market, or in the environment, from which you hope to benefit? Demographics, Economic, Political/legal, Sociological, Environmental, Technology and Cultural factors	What obstacles do you face? What are your competitors doing that may result in a loss of clients, customers, market share? Are the required specifications for your job, products or services changing? Is changing technology threatening your position?

Figure 1.2 SWOT

resources available. A development of a short-term strategy will help you bootstrap your new venture, but a longer-term strategy must also accompany it in order to make sure business continuity, growth, and a smooth transition can be expected. How detailed you make your own strategy depends upon the sufficiency with which you identified expected costs, complexity, and other potential obstacles, or anything that might bring the entire business plan to a screeching halt.

Since resources are limited and finite, you must establish priorities. What is the most crucial task or milestones to work on first and foremost? Where do the other milestones fall in the list of priorities? Compare and contrast your milestones with that of the competition. What will be your competitive edge that results in stealing customers away from your competitors? What strengths and opportunities can you capitalize on? Now that the strategy part of your business plan is complete, we need to slot in the tactics, the specific ways and means we will go about prosecuting and pursuing our strategic milestones.

Vision→Strategy→Tactics→Business Plan→Execution

Tactics are quick, actionable plans that take advantage of business opportunities as they arise. Tactics are the specifics in terms of the *how* to execute the strategy—details supporting the strategy. Tactics take the form of: *Who? What? How? When?* Each tactic will have its own profile and requirements in terms of:

- Resource requirements
- Risk involved in execution
- Costs
- Alignment with strategies, best practices, principles, and ethics

An example of a tactic compared to a strategy is "I intend to compete on the basis of price since my product is heavily commoditized," and the tactics involved include, "I need to find the means to reduce costs in terms of product, fulfillment, service, and administrative costs." The specifics answering your cost reduction efforts are then listed.

Figure 1.3 **Strategy**

At this point, we are ready to prepare our business plan. This plan isn't just for our own internal business planning. It will also be used to attract capital, to raise money. It will be the document that our sources of funds, such as banks or other financial institutions, use to judge the creditworthiness of our new business. Consequently, it must be good, it must be persuasive, it must be polished, it must be professional. Spend the time on it that it deserves because without the capital, there will be no business.

Some business plans are thick, highly detailed with technical appendices. The amount of information required will be a function of the product and market complexity and the amount of capital you seek to raise. For a small business, the plan should be relatively simple and easy to digest. Someone reading the document should be able to clearly understand all of the plan's information and to do so in less than an hour. Only disruptive innovators seeking hundreds of millions in commitments from say hedge funds, will go into greater detail, and only because the product and market strategies are truly unique, novel, and disruptive to the alternatives available today from our competitors.

What will the business plan contain? The plan is a guide, a roadmap, answering the question, "how will this business work?" and should start with an executive summary. For the busy financial executive, they demand this so they can quickly determine whether reading ahead even makes sense. From the summary, you then fold in the vision, strategy, and tactics in bullet-form or some easy-to-read format. Tables are used to list products, pricing, and these generally go in the back (appendices) along with pro forma (projected) financials. The financials can be simple, but should include at least a budget, projected sales, costs of running the business, cash flow (meaning you need to list items causing money to go out and money to come in), and required capital funding to meet the cash needs of the firm.

A one-page summary business plan, or executive summary, also known as a "lean" business plan will work when those from whom you seek to invest in the company are people you know, small lenders, or small amounts that can even be raised through crowdfunding. We will cover crowdfunding in greater detail in Chapter 3, "Raising the Money." Besides the vision, strategy, tactics, and SWOT, the business plan must include market demographic information, competition analysis, management team and experience, and other business specifics such as company location, facilities, technology, and regulatory environment.

Not to spend too much time and detail on the many business configuration possibilities in America, we first focus on some small online businesses that new entrepreneurs can pursue on the Internet with little or no startup capital. In the next chapter, we will move out of the "sheltering-in-place" state and into "hustles and side gigs." From there, we will explore raising capital (money) to run the business.

There are several kinds of online business models available, mainly focused on: product sales, advertisement revenue, or gathering specific data and turning it into information that others will pay for.

Table 1.1 Average dollar amount spend in millions on digital/mobile advertising by market sector 2019

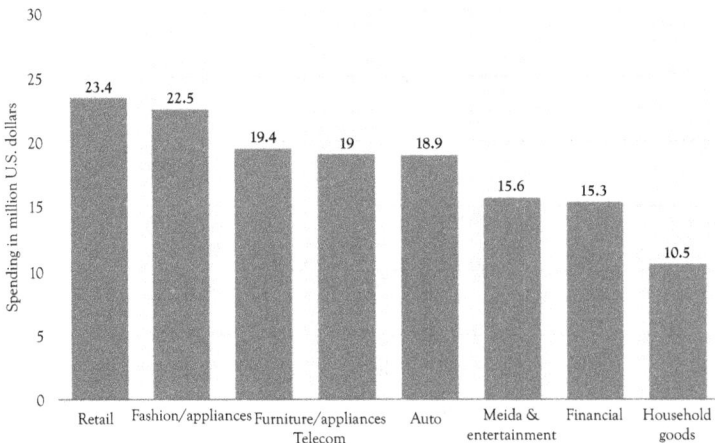

I have self-published my own book on Amazon. I have also created an online version of the finance course I taught at a local university. Other possibilities include:

- Create blogs, vlogs or products that can generate paid subscriptions once they become popular.
- Choose your subject, believing you have the background, expertise, and ideas to make this interesting.
- Select a blogging platform and register your domain.
- Locate and contact a web-hosting service.
- I recommend that you install WordPress for your blog.
- Step up to the plate and write your first blog.
- Point your e-mail connections, friends, and social media connects to the new blog with a link. Encourage feedback and comments.
- Once traffic is sufficient, you can begin to monetize your blog through paid membership.
- YouTube videos of almost anything that generates demand, from "how-to" to informational and entertaining.
  - Begin with your own personal YouTube video strategy
  - Make sure your video can be found on YouTube. Consider Search Engine Optimization (or SEO) when you create your video
  - Search for and explore related YouTube ideas and topics to get a feel of what generates popularity and just how you plan to make yours different, better, and more appealing
  - Understand YouTube equipment for beginners, start with your smartphone, upgrade later to a web camera, and only when success seems to be coming to you should you invest in professional gear
    a. Microphone
    b. Screen recorder
    c. Video editor
    d. Lighting
    e. Camera or webcam

- o Give serious consideration to an instructional video. According to the TechSmith study, 53 percent of people polled reported watching two or more instructional videos per week.[1]
- o Set up video recording equipment, record, and then edit
- o Upload your video to YouTube and optimize with annotations, titles, transitions, music, and other ideas to enhance the video appeal.

- Develop an app that no one else has thought about. We all have at times thought of a better app than the one on our smartphone, or even an entirely new app that will be popular and useful.

- Build a Shopify store. Shopify is a commercial platform that enables the creation of an online store. From physical and digital products to consulting and services, almost anything can be sold through your own customized Shopify store. A community built on sharing.

- Airbnb has been around more than a decade. Two designers who had extra space to share put up three travelers. Today, there are millions of hosts and millions of travelers that in the past had to pick a hotel or motel, now can choose where they want to stay and what kind of place they want to stay in. The Airbnb account is free, folks can list their space and book their unique accommodations and do so anywhere in the world 24 hours a day, 7 days a week. The Airbnb platform facilitates the collection and transfer of payments and verifies the personal profiles and listings, through a clever messaging system that both hosts and guests utilize to communicate questions and experiences. Airbnb promises help, facilitates refunds and reimbursements, and even offers insurance to the hosts so they won't worry about their property.

- Freelance pay per click consulting. Are you experienced in terms of subject matter expertise? Enough to get people to pay you for your advice? Consulting online is fast and easy, as people will pay for an answer to a legal question, for example. Rather than go to all the trouble of finding a lawyer and paying the lawyer a retainer.

If you have some skills that you believe others may need, you can hook up with a freelance network. What kind of skills? Writing and writing-related is the broadest category. If you already write a blog or articles on social media, you have honed your writing skills. You can help proofread and edit; you can offer services such as writing articles for existing web-based media. Magazines and newspapers still exist, but they are fast approaching obsolescence as online media are operating by taking on freelancers. Pick your favorite source of news, entertainment, editorial, and "how-to" and inquire how you might be a contributing writer.

- Sell products on eBay. This is a virtual and continuous garage sale that can generate income for someone who has a lot of things that they want to part with, and others might want to have.
- Web development—*if you are a good coder*—otherwise not for you.
- Copywriting, resumes, editing, and technical writing.
- B2B e-commerce or business-to-business electronic commerce to process orders digitally and improve transaction efficiencies between businesses.

These are some of the many possibilities that are especially attractive because you can get the business up and running quickly and for very little out-of-pocket. Taking your business online can be fun, inexpensive, and rewarding. Whether digital marketing, virtual selling, advertising, or the many other possibilities previously listed, you can find a niche that suits your interests, fits your passion, and leverages your experience and expertise. You can work from your home, utilize zoom conferencing to communicate with everyone involved in your new business, even host virtual events.

Case Study: YES THEORY

YES THEORY (https://yestheory.com). This is a brand built following the news of terror attacks. Thomas Brag (France), Ammar Kandil (Egypt), Matt Dajer (United States), an editor and a camera man, after a chance encounter in Montreal, Canada, utilized YouTube to create a unique brand with a message of inclusivity. They have been featured in media all over the world. Since early 2014, the video views have soared to almost 660 million and they boast 1.8 million Twitter followers.

The group portray foreign cultures in the spirit of authenticity, "consistently radiating positivity and promoting living life with an open mind, exactly what YouTube and the world needs."[2] When they first began, they were inspired to create a groundbreaking and novel video series that featured 30 things that they had never done before. From ear piercing to inventing a secret handshake with a mayor, this effort was aptly named *Project 30*.

Their angle is to actively seek to put themselves in uncomfortable, prickly and challenging situations, capturing picture profiles of inspiring people, amazingly heartwarming stories about strangers, exploring abandoned property, and many other fascinating adventures. Initially, they called their group **Generation Y Not**, but when Snapchat offered them the opportunity to make videos for pay, they left Montreal and moved to Venice, California and changed their name to Yes Theory.

In the spirit of growing their business through new products and interesting approaches, Yes Theory later launched the **Yes Theory Podcast**. It featured the group of three exploring the process of *self-improvement* to learn how people might pursue becoming their *truest selves*. Topics included such things as ego, vulnerability, and meditation. They partnered with **Headspace** cofounder Andy Puddicombe for *meditation*, then explored the nuances of *kindness* with Houston Kraft and Francois Clemmons, *burnout* with Anne Petersen, *physical discomfort* with Lauren Ash, *reinvention* with Rich Roll and Ryan Holiday, tackled *uncertainty* with Ozan Varol and Arthur Brooks, and delved into *novelty* with Jason Silva and Ben Nemtin.

Chris Corcoran, the Headspace Chief of Content commented, "We're thrilled to expand our slate of compelling, original content with Headspace, Yes Theory's inventive approach to life will resonate with listeners everywhere."

What does all this mean in financial terms? Yes Theory has a current estimated net worth of $3 million, not bad for three young guys. YouTube subscribers number over 6.5 million this year (2020) with

750 million views and counting. The channel averages 800,000 views per day and generates approximately $4,000 every single day, which translates into $1.5 million per year from the videos' ads. According to https://naibuzz.com[3]

> YouTubers get paid between $2 to $5 per 1000 monetized views after YouTube takes its cut. Monetized views range from 40%–60% of the total views. All these are influenced by several factors like device played on, the location of the viewer, ad inventory, how many ads there are on a video, how many people skip the ads, ad engagement, and so on. The cost of an ad view is based on an auction between advertisers based on views. Advertisers have to bid a minimum of $0.01 per view.

In addition to the ad revenue Yes Theory generates via YouTube, Yes Theory brings in money with brand deals through product promotions from companies such as Dollar Shave Club, SkyDive, and SkillShare. Yes Theory even sells their own merchandise under their brand, Seek Discomfort. For such a relatively small company with only three young men, they have created a multimillion-dollar business and are building and leveraging their brand. Brand is difficult to create, but it is one of those valuable assets you won't ever find listed on the balance sheet of a company's financial statements.

CHAPTER 2

Post-Pandemic: Beyond Internet—Gigs and Side Hustles

Throughout most of 2020, people were confined to their homes, sheltering in place. Though the government provided some assistance in the form of additional and extended unemployment benefits, and stimulus checks, a great many people were unable to return to their jobs, mostly confined to their homes for a large part of 2020. Many of their erstwhile jobs went from the status of temporary furlough to permanent layoff status as consumer demand cratered and companies sought to downsize and reduce their capacity to avoid the bankruptcies that were accelerating with the pandemic-induced recession.

In the previous chapter, we discussed Internet-based money-making opportunities that could be launched from home base and kept alive without the need to leave your home or apartment. This chapter we delve into the gigs and side hustles you can pursue outside your home now that the country is opening up again for business. The younger generations, particularly Millennials and Gen Z, mainly seek their own businesses, control over their own financial destiny, many eschew the thought of an office, a boss, and a corporate culture that requires mind-numbing meetings and little in the way of providing new and challenging tasks that leave workers with a sense of purpose and fulfillment.

Additionally, young people cannot afford to live in expensive cities where the best and highest paying jobs are located. This chapter covers many of the more recent and popular gigs and side hustles, most of which did not exist just a generation ago. These are money-making opportunities, some that require almost no skills whatsoever, just initiative, and some that will leverage the skills you may already possess. Pick one or more that suits your personality and passions. You can juggle multiple side hustles as they offer flexibility and can be pursued only a few hours a week or for as long as you want to work through each day, depending upon your own financial needs and your goals.

Media write a lot about booming tech, companies such as Amazon, Facebook, Netflix, Microsoft, Google, and others growing by leaps and bounds. But gigs and side hustles are growing even faster. You will not see that readily because these opportunities are so widely dispersed among a great many people. "Over the last few years, gig economy has seen accelerated growth and is a $100 billion industry with many businesses going digital thereby creating more online learning opportunities.

As per the research estimate, freelancing and gig working economy will be a $350 billion market by 2023. The Coronavirus pandemic has further boosted the gig working culture (remote working) and is likely to continue with market expansion at an unprecedented rate."[1]

Take care to evaluate each possible opportunity. Some of the sites want you to pay an upfront registration fee. You will also pay commissions or some part of the money you earn, for that is how the web business generates its own revenue. Be sure that whatever you are doing that you have insurance coverage. Not only car insurance for those gigs that involve driving your car, but liability insurance if something should go badly or you break things in someone else's home for example.

Most of these jobs will categorize you as an independent contractor. That means you buy your own health insurance, and at year-end, you will pay FICA taxes as a business owner rather than an employee. As an employee, the employer pays half the FICA taxes while the other half will be deducted from your paychecks. Finally, due care is required. I delivered meals for Meals-On-Wheels and some of the shut-ins wanted me to just walk right into their homes and put their food in the refrigerator because they were bed-ridden. That might be just a little too scary for most people.

Gigs and side hustles are jobs you do perhaps outside your primary fulltime job or could even be the only one or several money-making activities you have chosen for yourself. These gigs can be kind of fun, but most importantly, they are necessary to pay off debt or rebuild the savings you went through during the pandemic. The primary reason they can also be a lot fun is that they can be a means to tap and leverage your unused skills or explore passions. So, the first step is to assess your skills and capabilities. Here are a few examples to get you thinking about your own potential specialties that you might conceivably monetize:

- If you are multilingual, you are already advantaged as most Americans speak only English. You can teach English in the form of English-as-a-second-language or ESL. That teaching can be as simple as one-on-one or as elaborate as creating your own online class. Teaching English to foreigners can be done through places such as DaDaABC, Qkids, and Magic Ears if you best have a bachelor's degree and a personality that enjoys teaching others. The first require a degree, but Italki does not.

- Have you noticed how media loves to publish lists? *Ten Reasons to own Gold,* or *Five Metrics that show the Stock Market is Overpriced,* or *The Most Important Three Things you need to know about Dieting.* Now you can get paid for your own thoughtful and creative list. ListVerse (listverse.com) will pay you $100 for 1500 to 2000 words that are based upon a list of 10 items.

- Out from the pandemic, we are finally seeing a resurgence of events. Victor Marketing Agency (https://victory-agency.com/careers/) will hire you as their representative to host live events. Trade shows, new product promotions, sports, and entertainment events, their app will find gigs in your area. Their database has 40,000+ staff available, and work with companies of all sizes.

- MTurker (mturk.com) refers to Amazon's division of "crowd sourcing." Find and choose small jobs through their "marketplace." For example, a business needs people for data entry, so they post the "job" to the Mechanical Turk marketplace. You want it and select it, then you get paid via Paypal once your work has been approved by the business that needed the data entry. Companies seldom take longer than a day to approve the work.

Some of these gigs are quite granular. It could consist of typing the names, addresses and e-mail a company needs for which they will pay you 10 cents each. Or 20 cents to find a zip code for each address on a list (takes a bit longer). That doesn't sound like much, but over the course of a day's work you could bank as much as a hundred dollars.

- Bookkeeping and accounting are generally relatively easy to do and in high demand. You do not need a degree in accounting to perform entry-level accounting. Taking an online course will, however, help you with selling your credible credentials as capable. Bookkeepers.com will teach you freelance bookkeeping. This area is lucrative and can also lead to full-time positions if desired. The average bookkeeping freelancer is banking $300 per month.

- Do you love shopping? Then becoming a *mystery shopper* might be just the ticket for you. Check out BestMark (bestmark.com), Market Force (marketforce.com), and Secret Shopper (thesecretshopper.com). These companies cover a broad range of market research, from auditing and compliance to assessing the store staff behavior. They run the gamut and can hire you for surveys, monitoring social media or running a focus group.

- If you well know the area in which you live, including the not-so-well known hidden-away spots, and have learned the rich history of your town, you might want to sign up to be a tour guide. Crowd Work News (crowdworknews.com) is the site that will get you started. You may be surprised at how popular tours can be. I avoided tours until I was forced to go on one in London with a colleague. Sitting on top of the double-decker bus the tour guide spoke about buildings that had been bombed in WWII and all kinds of fascinating trivia I had never heard before. I was hooked.

Figure 2.1 Tours

Car as a Means to Make Money

Your car can be your most valuable asset in the gig economy. Ride-share companies, the biggest of which are Uber and Lyft, need drivers. To become a ride-share driver, you only need be 21-years old with one to three years of driving experience, possess a driver's license, car insurance, and produce your vehicle registration. Additionally, your care needs to be a four-door vehicle that can seat five people. A criminal and driving background check will also be a part of the hiring process.

The amount of money you will make as a ride-share driver varies depending on how often you are willing to drive and what time of day. Peak time driving can result in putting more money in your pocket. This is one of the best side hustles for people who seek the control over their schedule and how much money they make.

Related is the food delivery side hustle. If you have a car, that hopefully is reliable and gets good gas mileage, you can deliver the food customers are ordering by phone or online from restaurants. This job boomed when restaurants were no longer serving at their locations and could only offer curbside service or delivery to their customers. Many restaurants were so hard hit by this sudden drop in business that they went bankrupt, along with a wave of other customer-facing businesses from entertainment to salons.

Typical pay runs about $18 an hour and you can choose your own flexible schedule when you want to be available to deliver food orders. Uber Eats (https://ubereats.com) and Door Dash (https://doordash.com) are just two food delivery opportunities that you can reach by downloading their apps to your smartphone. In addition to these third-party apps, you can contact your local eateries, such as pizzerias, to see if they need part-time drivers.

For Uber, the food delivery business is more profitable than the ride hailing business they have. This resulted from the pandemic, when people were fearful of anything like public transportation, while they also did not want to venture out to find meals. Today, Uber is large and growing fast, generating billions in revenue, and continuing to add more and more restaurants to their app.

Figure 2.2 Global food delivery services market[2]

Instacart (Instacart.com) allows app-based online shopping from home and hires people to deliver the groceries to them. Shoppers can order for same-day delivery or up to two weeks in advance. The shopping angle separates Instacart from other delivery competitors in the gig and hustle economy, companies like Door Dash and Uber Eats, although Door Dash and Postmates are trying hard to break into the grocery store business. Instacart can be found in most major metropolitan areas, so if you live in Los Angeles, New York, Miami, or dozens of other densely populated areas of the country, you can sign up to deliver. Instacart is making plans to take the company public in 2021 with a value well over $10 billion.

Selling Your Crafts

Perhaps the greatest threat to all these gigs and side hustles is Amazon muscling in on their turf. If this concerns you then consider partnering with Amazon, knowing that this predator finds a way to make whatever they want work as a successful business. Amazon Handmade, or Handmade at Amazon, is an online store within the Amazon store and marketplace that is customized for artisans. Much like Etsy, Amazon Handmade offers sellers the chance to sell handcrafted, and one-of-a-kind creations. It has, unsurprisingly, become one of the top ecommerce businesses in the past few years. Categories include clothing, jewelry, pet accessories, artwork, and anything else people's creative genius can dream up. The only requirement is that these items be "hand-made." You must first apply, and this requires a description of what you make and how you make it, perhaps include some photos, the whole process can be finished in a half hour or so.

Somewhat similar to Etsy (see the following Table 2.1), you will pay a 15 percent commission on your sales. If you are already on Etsy, that doesn't preclude you from also listing on Amazon Handmade. This will result in reaching many more customers as Amazon Handmade boasts almost 100 million U.S. customers and 250 million worldwide. Many people know and trust Amazon, so this is a distinct advantage over the smaller Etsy. One disadvantage, however, is that for Amazon Handmade you must make your products in advance and ship to an Amazon warehouse, so that precludes you from selling these anywhere else.

Table 2.1 Amazon Handmade versus Etsy[3]

Amazon Handmade	ETSY
Selling 40 items	Selling 40 items
Average cost: $18 per item	Average cost: $18 per item
Average shipping: $6 per item	Average shipping: $6 per item
12% transaction fee	3.5% transaction fee + 3% payment fee
$40 monthly fee per seller	$0.2 listing fee per item
$960 in total Revenue	$960 in total Revenue
$155.20 in fees	$54.80 in fees
16.2% of revenue	5.7% of revenue

Handyman and Odd Jobs

Leah Busque Solivan was out of dog food and it was late, she thought how wonderful it would be if she could find a service that would get the dog food and deliver it to her. That was the beginning of a new iPhone app called TaskRabbit. Between that late night and today, Busque Solivan built a business that has grown to 44 cities while raising more than $50 million from venture capitalists.

Are you skilled and like to hop around doing different odd and handyman jobs? TaskRabbit might be just the thing for you. I have had furniture delivered that I had to assemble. At least twice that I can remember, I destroyed the desk or whatever and had to carry the pieces out and throw them in the dumpster. Take a look at TaskRabbit.com. There you will see examples of skilled people in terms of their number of positive reviews, number of tasks completed, and how much they charge per hour per task. Somewhat surprisingly, these taskers can make up to $100 an hour doing repairs in your home and helping you move.

The tasks include almost anything you need to get done but fear you lack the knowledge and/or skills to do it yourself. You can save a lot of money using these taskers rather than professionals advertising through Yelp or showing up on search engines. This can be a lucrative side hustle for the skilled plumber or electrician, the computer nerd, or gardener/landscaper. Besides TaskRabbit, you can find similar sites such as Handy (Handy.com). Many taskers claim to be earning upwards of $2,000 per week!

Care for a Creature

Another gig that appeals to many with a kind heart is caring for a creature, from a child to the elderly, and even pets. The trick with this is that you avoid the expensive and time-consuming regulations of running a nursing home or a day-care center. As the U.S. population is aging and social media and pandemics are leaving many lonely and hungering for social relationships, many opportunities have opened up. Work-from-home parents need you to take their kids to the park. Someone needs care for their elderly parent because they are going on a long vacation. Doctor's appointments and other reasons to have to leave the house mean someone has to watch those left in the house.

Pet care is in high demand as well. Checking in on Shadow the Labrador, taking her to the vet or just a nice walk while the owner is at work can mean money for part-time work. You can add on services such as a bath, cleaning the ears, trips to the vet, or practicing new tricks and better behavior.

The common denominator in all of these side hustles is you are providing mobility and convenience to those who cannot or do not want to leave their homes and would prefer to pay someone to do the things that must get done. We all think of businesses like landscaping and delivering food when we think of mobility. But your opportunity is to take the service that used to be only offered from a physical location and converting them to get the same thing via mobile apps. For example, you are making yourself available in such a way that you get a call to go to someone's home, cut their hair, groom their dog, and wash their car. With the selection of sites and apps we listed earlier, the sky is the limit and only your time, energy, and flexibility will impede you. The convenience factor is a huge plus, but you are offering a service to those who might still be hesitant about going out and doing these simple chores in a post-Covid world. The virus has changed culture radically.

Long ago, the Great Depression changed the culture and in turn changed the mainstream behavior. The economic collapse turned people toward saving more money, using less debt, and assimilating the virtue of frugality. Likewise, the COVID-19 pandemic turned those who had adopted the *debt is good* view of financial matters toward understanding that all debt really does is cannibalize your future standard of living by providing the enjoyment of a standard of living today that exceeds earnings. "Debt is the worst poverty."[4]

CHAPTER 3

Raising the Money

Moving beyond the sheltering-in-place at home gigs of Chapter 1, and the side hustles outside the home that required little of your own money to get started, in Chapter 2, we turned to the larger and more sophisticated business ventures. Chapter 3 explains how you raise the funds to start your own business. We covered business planning, so the Business Plan is the starting point because in it you have determined how much cash to start your business, and how much additional cash going forward will be needed to run the ongoing business. The next chapter, Chapter 4, will give you the guidance for running that business, but first things first.

Cash is the lifeblood of any business, for without it, the business is insolvent and either files for bankruptcy or simply can no longer provide customers with your products or services. (We will cover the two broadest forms of business, manufacturing in Chapter 6 and service businesses in Chapter 7.)

This may come as a surprise to some, but a successful, growing, and profitable business can become bankrupt if it runs out of cash and has no means of raising additional cash. We cannot overemphasize the importance of sufficient capital along with the available avenues to raise more capital if and when needed. This chapter will begin with modest capital requirements for a new small business and end with a case of how a successful company went out of business because of their cash flow issues.

Savings and Credit Cards

Many a small business was started in a garage with only one or few people pooling together a little cash and perhaps using their credit cards. The risk of course is that if the business is never significant and profitable that you will be wiped out in terms of your savings and have to get job working for a company to get your credit card balances paid off. The beauty is that you, along with your partners, are the sole heirs to the fruits of your labor, as the business owners. Most of what will require cash is probably obvious. Money for a business license, any equipment you need, and if a manufacturing business the cost of labor, materials, outside contractors, and overhead. Overhead can include utilities, rent and other supplies, and administrative costs. To take this route, you need a reasonable assurance that the business will produce a product that will (a) generate customer demand at a growing rate, and (b) provide price points and revenue that after all the costs leave you with profit.

With a new business, you may have big dreams but if you want to reduce your risk you need to start small. Frugality and careful control of cash will be paramount, particularly until you get to the point where you have a good amount of new orders from paying customers to replenish the cash coffers. While you don't want to stifle your growth, and you certainly don't want to cede your growing market share to your competitors, you don't want to bite off more than you can chew and find yourself suddenly out of funding.

Friends and Family

Uncle Bob believes in your new venture and is willing to loan you some money, just as a couple of friends from college have promised to do. How do you receive their investments? What will be the structure? You have two basic choices in front of you. First, you can give them a share of the new company and they will become shareholders just as you and your partners. Though silent in running the business, if the value of the company quadruples quickly, not unlikely if you started from scratch, you hand over a big windfall to Uncle Bob.

An alternative is to structure Uncle Bob's investment as a loan. Perhaps he trusts you and therefore is not asking for collateral or assets to pledge, and hopefully, the interest rate would be low and the due date for repayment far enough in the future that it won't present a cash flow problem. A simple promissory note that you will repay Uncle Bob in two years' time at 5 percent interest should suffice. One other creative approach for those who are excited about your business and the products would be—instead of interest—pay them back in products and/or services if that makes sense to them.

Crowdfunding

Crowdfunding is a relatively new source of raising money for almost any purpose, from a new business to providing funds for the medical care of an afflicted friend who perhaps has no health insurance. Crowdfunding leverages small amounts from a large number of individuals to bootstrap your new business venture. Crowdfunding will make use of the accessibility of networks of people through websites and social media. This fundraising choice brings investors together with entrepreneurs.

There are today a variety of general and specialized (niche) crowdfunding sites to raise money. We will cover the top seven:

1. Kickstarter—The target location is global. It is a rewards-based business model that charges 5 percent of the funds raised. It appeals to small businesses and aspiring entrepreneurs. Techies and artists like it and the *games* category has reached almost a quarter billion dollars annually.
2. Indiegogo—Similar to Kickstarter in terms of the global location, rewards-based model and 5 percent charge, it appears to be competing head-on with Kickstarter.

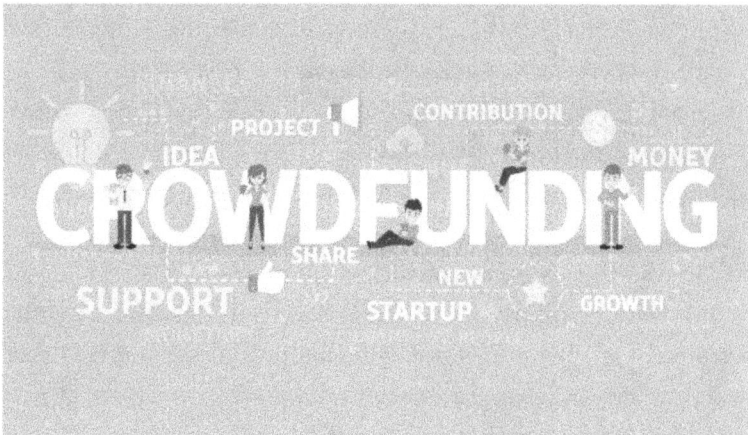

Figure 3.1 Crowdfunding

3. GoFundMe/Crowdrise[1]—Big and generated $5 billion in funds just this past decade. It is a donations-based model and aimed primarily at *personal causes* of individuals and groups such as the Las Vegas Victims Fund where it raised almost $12 million, but many startup businesses have utilized GoFundMe.

4. Crowdfunder—Crowdfunder is an equity crowdfunding platform for sourcing and funding ventures and boasts a large network— over 130,000 entrepreneurs and investors. With an average deal size of just under $2 million, venture capital (private equity) firms troll here to vet and approve their investments in startups, so this site expects well-thought-out and compelling business propositions to pique their interest.

5. SyndicateRoom—This is a venture capital fund based in the UK (Cambridge). If you are starting your new business in the UK, this should be the first fund-raising site you visit.

6. Crowdcube/Seedrs (Two companies merged October 2020)[2]— Also UK-based, this outfit was inspired following the last recession, when tough times made raising new venture capital exceedingly difficult. As we are once again coming out of yet another recession, this company is great for checking all the boxes in terms of what your UK venture is going to need: legal and compliance, marketing, engineering, product design, and finance. Seedrs had raised over $1 trillion in funding and done over 1,000 deals.

7. KissKissBankBank (seriously)—Named after the 2005 film Kiss Kiss Bang Bang, KissKissBankBank is a collaborative financing company based in France; it's been in business for a decade now. A similar model as Kickstarter, it is one of Europe's leading crowdfunding sites with more than 31,000 projects.

Crowdfunding will not only help you raise the needed capital, but the side benefit is all the attention and free advertising. You are raising awareness of your new business. All your social media connections should be sought and encouraged to comment and share your post, thereby reaching all your connections' connections.

RAISING THE MONEY   27

Other Loans

Next up in the hierarchy of raising capital are loans. Loans can be structured as either personal or a business loan. This is where your new business plan will be tested. Your bank will look at the usual metrics such as your credit history (FICO) and whether your credit report contains any "adverse" accounts. They will also want to understand your ability to repay the loan and that is why the financial portion of your business plan must be solid. Finally, the lender will ask for collateral. Collateral are assets they attach, put a lien on, and will take in lieu of nonpayment. New businesses sometimes need to go deep into debt, with some entrepreneurs taking a second mortgage on their homes to get the money they need. Better be sure you will be able to service this loan or both business and possibly home could be lost if you cannot make your payments.

A good way to structure financing is to remember that long-term debt is best matched against long-term obligations. Likewise, short term with short-term obligations. What that simply means is that you get a 5-year loan, for example, for the long-term cash needs of the company, and a credit line that you can tap for the ups and downs of your cash balance that changes with the cash cycle. The cash cycle can be short or long. Most companies deliver goods or services and invoice with 30-days allowed for payment. But if your business is taking payment in the form of a credit card, you will actually generate cash flow as you grow. This is just one of many competitive advantages that Amazon has going for it.

SBA's and NGO's (Small Business Administration and Nongovernment Organizations)

During the pandemic, the government passed the CARES Act. The Coronavirus Aid, Relief, and Economic Security (CARES) Act was passed by Congress with wide support and signed by the president in late 2020. Providing $2 trillion in economic relief, the money went to American workers, their families, and small businesses. As of this writing, the government is continuing to come up with additional economic stimulus so more small business capital conduits are likely to become available in 2021 even with the new administration.

The SBA does not itself provide the loans. What it does is work with the lenders to process your application and provide the loan if you meet their credit requirements. Those requirements are what you might expect: no criminal background, good credit (FICO over 740 would be ideal), no past loan (e.g., student) or loan defaults, and not a lot of unencumbered assets that might represent money spent unnecessarily elsewhere. You have options looking for the right lender, finding a lender by searching yourself or using a referral service. Referral services such as SmartBiz (https://smart-bizloans.com) are helpful for the new or relatively new businesses that are not experienced when it comes to working with lenders, or if you just don't have the time yourself to do a good search.

Starting a Nongovernmental Organization (NGO) because you want to fight for a cause, or advocate or solve some problem can be initially very exciting usually. However, your effort requires funding. First you need to raise awareness about the work you intend. That can be through TV, radio, social media, friends, the people for whom you advocate, related organizations, and other ways to promote the cause such as the printing of T-shirts for employees and stakeholders. Writing articles and seeking to publish the advocacy need will also get the word out, raise awareness and hopefully raise money. Here are some basic steps to take with your NGO:

1. Start by making a website, that is always a best starting point for all businesses.
2. Bring together like-minded enthusiasts and form a group, referring to them as members, mentors, advocates, and so on.
3. With your new group, develop your business plan so you have a shared vision and strategy that can work as a team to get the word out. Social media and networking, along with building a referral system will take hard work and a lot of reaching out and spreading the word.
4. Partner with businesses to sponsor you. Whether that means just leaving flyers in their place of business, or better yet, getting funding and support, this step is foundational and can mean

the difference between success and failure. Offer to advertise the business in your own marketing collateral and communications.

5. Since your NGO can be termed as a *cause*, getting political figures on board and involved should be part of the strategy. In addition, these people can assist in whatever government support you can get.

6. Create a *hit list* of places where you will go to proclaim your mission: communities, churches, schools, workplaces, even door-to-door with your staff to raise money. Support boxes at each place, including your business partners, will also help.

Having covered the most direct and common ways of getting cash, the lifeblood of your new and small company, we will move up into the changing capital needs of the larger and ongoing business. This remains pertinent to the new entrepreneur because it is almost certain your expectation is that you will become larger and you plan to be a going concern. The areas we cover now are more sophisticated, so the approach must match the level of sophistication. As a small business owner, you may not even recognize some of the terminology, so consider this your first cursory foray into the world of high finance.

Private Equity

Private equity (PE) is ownership or interest in a company not publicly listed or traded. The difference between what are referred to as private equity versus venture capital is this: The investments in private companies by investors is called *private equity*. With private equity, investments come in at a later stage of business growth and expansion, whereas *venture capital* is an investment made in the earlier stages (also called *seed* or *startup capital*).

As another source of investment capital, private equity (PE) originates with high net-worth individuals and firms who then take stakes, that is, ownership interests, in private companies or also could be seeking to acquire control of a certain target public company with plans to take that company private (which means they will be delisted from the stock exchange where their stock formerly traded).

The PE industry is made up of institutional investors: pension funds, large PE firms funded by investors. Because PE involves direct investment, in order to gain control over the company operations, a significant amount of capital is required, which is why these funds are so large.

The minimum capital requirement for accredited investors varies, depending on the firm and on the type of fund. You can find some funds with a $250,000 minimum entry requirement; others may require millions. The fee structure for PE firms typically has both a management and a performance fee component. One example, though this varies, is a yearly management fee of 2 percent of the assets, plus 20 percent of the gross profit earned at the time the company is sold.

Management oversight makes up the second major function of PE professionals. Among the support they will be giving, the firm is teaching and training a young executive staff best practices in terms of strategic planning and financial management. They typically try to eliminate administrative inefficiencies and streamline and simplify new accounting, purchasing, IT systems, and other overhead tasks.

How do you source PE? It will be best if you look to the firms that have done deals in the past with businesses as close in size, complexity, and type of business as your own. That way you know they have the experience, and you can also tap the references for feedback. But be careful. The individuals in these firms are the best and the brightest in finance. They are trying to make their best deal, so you need to be ready to negotiate on every aspect, metric, and cost that they propose to you.

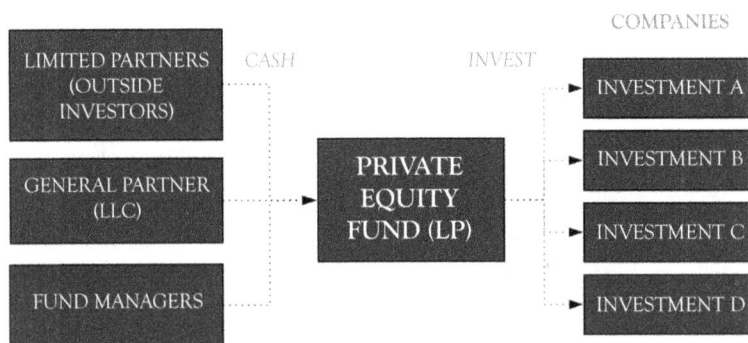

Figure 3.2 Private equity

Stocks and Bonds

Selling stock in your company can be done privately or publicly, but either way you are giving an ownership interest in your company in exchange for capital needed to grow. This decision should be put off as long as possible, since down the road, a stock you gave up for $10 may be worth $100 in the not-too-distant future. There is a sweet spot, an optimal relationship or ratio between the equity (stock) and the debt (loans, bonds, etc.). The more debt you have, also known as *other people's money*, the greater your own return as you carefully guard the ownership among yourself and the original partners in the firm.

But too much debt can topple any company, even the profitable ones. One of the hallmarks of today's culture is that *debt is good*. Debt in the right mix can indeed be good. But debt is like steroids, a little can do a lot but too much will destroy. The problems many firms have run into today is that when our monetary authorities (Federal Reserve) sought to bring down interest rates, that created a low-cost loan scenario that made debt appear affordable on all the levels. Government, corporations, and households have binged on debt without realizing the price they will ultimately pay comes later and could hit harder.

For the first time in American history, we have the so-called *zombie* companies. These are companies that are technically insolvent, but they remain afloat only by successively refinancing their overload of debt. And monetary and fiscal programs reach out to them to ensure they don't go under. This has led to inefficiencies in the allocation of capital, since capital no longer flows smoothly to the best, most efficient, and highest returning investments. Many zombies will quickly collapse and expire if (when?) interest finally return to market levels that impute risk premiums.

Bonds are company IOU's that investors snap up today at very low interest rates. That makes financing appear to argue for more and more sales of bonds since the interest expense won't be too much of a burden for the company to carry. A great many companies are even selling bonds for no other purpose than to repurchase their own stock in order to reward their stock-option holding executive suite and provide shareholders a windfall while avoiding the double-taxation of paying dividends on the stock.

When all the monetary and fiscal intrusions finally disappear, and it is unclear how and when that might be, the companies with large debt loads will be the first to become insolvent. They will scramble to refinance given the breakeven points are too high with high debt service. But as they do so, they will find the imputation of a risk premium has returned, and the corporate death spiral will be well underway. The prudent course is to be very careful when it comes to how much debt the company can swallow and be less greedy about giving up some ownership in the company. Finally, a sizable cash balance is a good hedge because although this particular recession may be disappearing in the rear-view mirror, we can be certain another one will hit again in the future.

CHAPTER 4

Running the Business

Running a business today is radically different than just 10 years ago. Millennials and Gen Z are culturally different than Baby Boomers. The thought of working in an office for a large company until retirement is abhorrent to many of them. They are not as driven to work hard, long hours, save as much as they can, marry, have a family, and buy a house. For most of them, some or even all of these goals and objectives are far from being termed *personal priority*.

That creates two new challenges. First, for the long-time incumbent businesses, how do they attract and retain this new breed of worker? And secondly, for these young people, what should their aspirations and goals be for their own lives? We will attempt to bridge these two *new normal* conditions, for today companies and workers alike are unsure and unclear what matters most and what might they do to be successful.

Begin with the younger entrepreneurs who are at least relatively new at running a business. They have been immersed into the world of commerce, cash flow, profitability, creditors, partners and shareholder/owners, regulatory compliance, and all in the context of a highly competitive environment that is changing so fast that today's latest must have product could go by the wayside in a very short period of time.

America has changed and a lot of the change has been challenging, even problematic. Public schools no longer prepare students for colleges and universities they cannot afford anyway. Companies complain they are not getting the requisite skills they need for success from those who do mortgage themselves to the hilt to get a college degree. Starting with big tech companies—these are now testing applicants for their potential. If they show a spark of initiative, some creativity, and ability to think critically and systematically, they get hired without any degree. The company then educates and trains them both while they are being paid. Inhouse courses complemented by courses at the local university are all paid for by the company.

This trend will continue and took a great leap forward when the pandemic forced all the schools of higher education to essentially move from a campus environment to online. With this new model, the glaringly high tuition no longer meets the cost-benefit calculation for many would be students. Individuals are figuring out that they can learn precisely the things and skills they want to obtain online. YouTube offer hundreds of tutorials and specifically tailored courses that will fit precisely with personal education goals. It will be a while before the majority of the big companies finally put a stop to certain degrees and certification requirements, but that is the direction we are heading in today.

Here is a list of 14 companies that no longer require a degree, along with some of their current open positions[1]:

1. Google—Network Specialists, Software Engineer, Contracts Manager, Sales Management, Digital Marketing, Hardware Engineering, Business Intelligence, Account Strategy, Technical Programs
2. Ernst & Young (currently UK only)—Tax Senior and Tax Services, Advisory Services, Consultant, Machine Learning Engineer, Transfer Pricing, International Tax, Financial Services Manager - Penguin Random House Design Fellowship, Postproduction, Accounts Payable, Publicists, Imprint Sales, Editorial Assistant, Design, Marketing Assistant, Director of Operations, Social Media Marketing, Senior Web Designer
3. Costco Wholesale—Stock, Warehouse Order Picker, Pharmacy Tech, Optometrist, Optician, Advanced Analytics, Membership Assistant, SAP Quality Assurance, Cashier, IT Portfolio Manager, Software Engineer
4. Whole Foods—Store Cashier, Grocery Team, Cake Decorator, Rotational Team, Meat Cutter, Specialty Beverage, Produce Team, Floral Team, Packaged Software Engineer, Software Development Engineer, Salesforce Administrator
5. Hilton—Events and Catering, Security Officer, Room Attendant, Front Desk, Executive Chef, Front Office, Senior Staff Accountant, Sales Representative, Manager of Talent and Rewards, Night

Auditor, Director of Human Resources, Hotel Manager, Food and Beverage Manager

6. Publix—CRM Data Analyst, Consumer Insights Projects, Business Analyst, Manager of GIS and Locations, Warehouse Selector, Marketing Analytics Consultant, Pharmacist, SQA Analyst, Grocery, Business Consultant, Maintenance, Net Development, Fuel Truck Operator, Cloud Architect

7. Apple—Developer Tools Engineer, Account Executive, Specialist, Siri Site Engineer, Technical Support, GIS Tech, Full Stack Engineer, Research Scientist, Ops Supervisor, Demand Planner, System Software Engineer, Education Development

8. Starbucks—Baristas, Shift Super, Store Managers, Financial Analyst, Manager of Partner and Asset Protection, Senior Auditor, Accountant, Marketing Manager of Innovation, Brand Manager, Market Research and Insights Manager, Product Manager, Associate Project Manager

9. Nordstrom—Salesperson, Site Reliability Engineer, Retail Sales, Loss Prevention, Host, Beauty Counter Manager, Head Cashier, Wedding Stylist, Strategy Program Manager, Senior Vendor Manager, Department Manager, Director of Corporate Strategy, Database Administrator, Senior Web Engineer

10. Home Depot—Department Supervisor, Customer Service, Cashier, Assistant Store Manager, Outside Sales Consultant, Warehouse Assoc, Product Manager, Analyst, Employment Marketing Specialist, Lead Generation Manager, Senior Analyst of SEO, UX Designer, Systems Engineer Manager, Field Staffing Manager, Strategic Sourcing Lead

11. IBM—Data Scientist, Privacy Analyst, Technology Program Manager, Software Engineer, Digital Marketing Manager, Research Staff, Managing Consultant, Research Scientist, Blockchain Engineer, Lead Recruiter, Contract and Negotiations Professional, Product Manager, Entry Level System Services Representative, Research Staff, Client Solution Executive

12. Bank of America—Admin Assistant, Private Wealth Assoc, Visual Designer, Lending Associate, Investment Analyst, Quantitative Finance, Relationship Banker, Lead Svc Designer, Client Svc

Representative, Client Associate, Executive Assistant, Relationship Manager, Consumer Banking Market Manager, Treasury Analyst, Small Business Consultant

13. Chipotle—District Manager, Kitchen Manager, Service Manager, Restaurant Team, General Manager, Restaurant Shift Leader, Accounts Payable, Financial Accountant, Brand Activation Manager, Litigation Paralegal, Senior Counsel

14. Lowe's—Merchandising Support Technical Analyst, Network Engineer, IT S/W Engineer, Employee Relations, Network Voice Engineer, Content Manager, Lead Brand Advocate, Merch Marketing Analyst, Sales Specialist, Plumbing Associate, Commercial Sales Loader, Lumber Associate, Front End Cashier, Internet Fulfillment, Seasonal Customer Svc Associate, Delivery Puller, Installed Sales Manager

The trend today is away from higher education. Some career fields require a college degree for they require certifications. But unless you want to be a lawyer, a public accountant, or a doctor, the degree prerequisite is fast disappearing. Even STEM and science can be learned through Internet sites like YouTube, tuned to precisely the content and subject matter you want to pursue.

Your business must have as its company slogan, first and foremost, *"blessed are the flexible, for they shall not be broken."* All of what was required in the past is either questionable, can be substituted for, or can be done without entirely. Your location can be virtual, it doesn't even need to be your garage or your home. Your employees, likewise, can work from where they choose for many jobs, except of course the customer-facing jobs for which every service business needs a location and equipment.

WeWork (wework.com) is a commercial real estate company providing shared workspaces for tech startups. Headquartered in New York City, WeWork manages almost 5 million square yards. A popular shared working spaces business, WeWork made a name for themselves by giving small businesses and entrepreneurs a path to success in business. With spaces all over the world, WeWork is at the core simply an office-leasing company. It makes money renting office space. WeWork purchases real estate, sometimes only a single floor in an office building, then transforms it into small offices with common areas. It rents desks to individuals who want the benefits that come from a fully stocked office without having to shell out a lot of money for a full office.

Members are independent freelancers, remote workers, folks that need an occasional office. They generally require unlimited Wi-Fi. And other customers include small businesses with several employees needing a place to go and work, to conduct meetings, building their business while watching the costs. This is a good location model for the entrepreneur that has a business bigger than a basement but small enough to seek flexible real estate at affordable rates.

As I was finishing up my own career, Millennials were coming into the workplace, so I was fortunate enough to be able to carefully observe their behaviors, personalities, and the things they seemed to want and like and others they didn't care much about and did not like. You cannot generalize on any generation, but you can identify patterns. Since I was in tech and the cutting edge of cool and progressive, the companies I knew offered ping-pong, free food, nap rooms, even kegs of beer. But that did not matter to them nearly as much as having a role that provided meaning for their lives, flexibility for their schedules, and a good salary.

They aspired to work with other smart people in order to learn from them and be challenged to become more knowledgeable themselves. They were not clock watchers and appreciated a lot of flexibility in terms of coming in, taking off for appointments and even what time they left work. They did personal things like online shopping and banking during working hours, but evenings and weekends they answered e-mails from bosses and colleagues, so the morphing of job and private life created a blur and the traditional 9 to 5 no longer made any sense whatsoever.

With the wealth gap widening today, over half of Americans are not making sufficient salary to ever own a home. It is certainly understandable that they seek higher compensation. When they read that the CEO of their company took over a hundred million in compensation, while they may have earned only $30,000, we can expect resentment to build. This is one of the reasons young people are being drawn to socialism today. In their view, the capitalist model is broken, for the vast majority of the wealth and income is in the hands of a single-digit percentage of Americans.

Running Your Business

The cultural shifts and most recently the pandemic have changed a lot of the dynamics when it comes to successfully running a business. Most books like this one would advise watching cash flow closely, for without cash, it is "game over." The advice would delve into financial ratios and metrics, maintaining a dashboard that provides daily a refresh of new orders, shipments and revenue, gross margin, cost of sales, and operating expenses. That is still as valuable as it ever was, but this chapter focuses more on what has markedly changed in the recent past and what must be done to adjust to the times in order to keep your business running successfully.

There is a myth that today's younger workers will only stay a couple years, leverage what they have been trained for and through experience can do, and move on to another company and a better job. That is untrue. Research shows that globally, employees today aspire to build long-term careers with one company. They want to find the company where they will feel they fit, they belong, and will make a commitment. Shared purpose, shared values, shared mission, they simply want to be a part of a growing and successful business.

median tenure with current employer

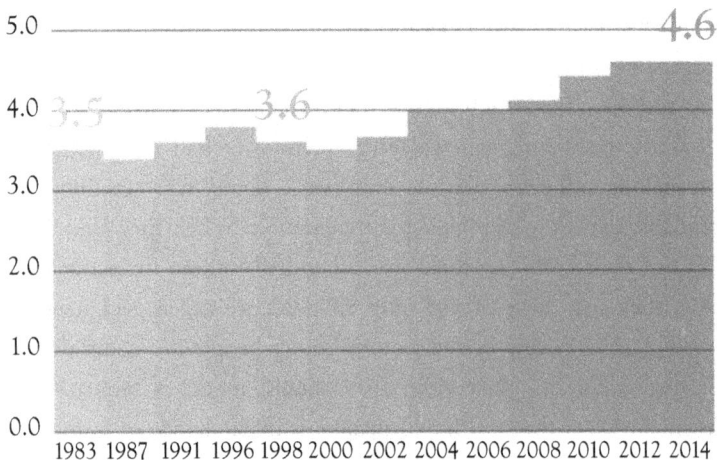

Figure 4.1 *Median tenure with current employer*

What does that mean for how you approach human resources? It means you can still attract and retain good people. Contrary to what we read about today's lack of loyalty, both on the part of the employer and the employee, is simply untrue. So cast that aside and consider—from a cultural standpoint—what a new employee wants and expects.

I worked for a high-tech global manufacturing company and was impressed with the CEO's basic philosophy. He never sought to "delight the customer," as MBA courses and seminars always stress. Rather, he sought to earn loyalty and respect by treating his suppliers and employees well.

Employees: Well compensated. Treated fairly. Flexible schedules. Personal tasks allowed to be done at work. Celebrating success together.

Suppliers: Trust. Fair. Long-term relationships that gave most of the business to one or maybe two suppliers, in spite of the conventional wisdom to have more qualified suppliers. Never wavering on a commitment, even those that were not written into purchase orders and contracts. If a dispute arose, the CEO generally allowed that the supplier was right and thus responded accordingly, delighting the supplier.

It turned out to be the winning formula, as Southern California's Kingston Technology was the most sought-after company to work for and do business with. The customers, throughout 125 countries, were highly satisfied with Kingston's USB's, SSD (Solid State Drives), and DRAM modules (dynamic random-access memory). The CEO, David Sun, built the private company into a $10 billion per year behemoth, and became one of Forbes wealthiest billionaires.

Turn now to *corporate social responsibility* (CSR). As social media began to threaten the profligate and scofflaw companies by posting unflattering reviews of products and business practices, companies responded with efforts aimed at demonstrating that they were in business for more than just making a profit. The evolution from a plaque in conference rooms, extolling company virtues, principles, and ethics, that most people simply smiled at, company websites updated their pages to include corporate social responsibility.

The task of creating this new page on the website generally fell with the IT organization. That effort consisted of transcribing the conference room plaque claims into the website for all to read and hopefully realize the company deserved to be seen as having high integrity and following honest and fair business practices rather than predatory and sketchy behavior. Over time, companies hired experienced web content employees with good marketing skills and the CSR page was updated, expanded, and covered subjects ranging from climate change to community involvement. It all sounded great, altruistic, and now another relatively new business challenge could be said to have been fully met and met well.

It did not quite work out that way. If companies behaved badly, their CSR notwithstanding, social media would pounce. The modern-day equivalent of an angry mob was the worst thing that could happen to any business, damaging their brand and making things tough in terms of damage control. Now we turn to three examples of companies that have all but managed to destroy themselves for lack of good, sound, ethical strategic decisions.

The Hertz Corporation is an American car rental company that operates in 10,200 locations internationally. As one of the largest U.S. car rental companies by sales and fleet size, Hertz owns Dollar and Thrifty. In 2019, the company had revenues of almost $10 billion, assets of $25 billion, and close to 40,000 employees.

In May 2020, the company filed for bankruptcy, citing a pandemic-related decline in revenue and future bookings. The new ride-hailing Uber and Lyft did not help them either. Hertz stumbled along the way to oblivion. Long before the pandemic, Hertz was already drowning in debt. Over 90 percent of the firm's capital consisted of $19 billion in debt.

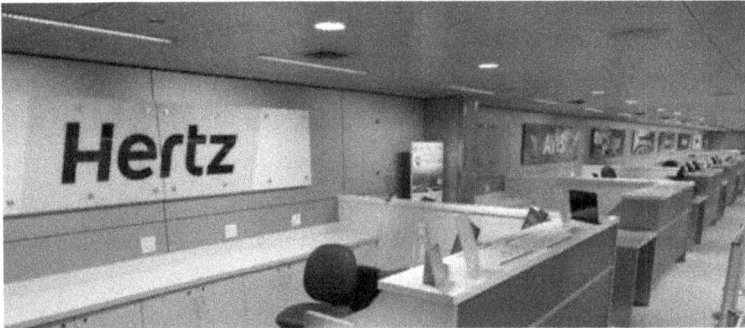

Figure 4.2 The Hertz corporation

In June 2020, Hertz (HTZ) plotted what could have been one of history's greatest bankruptcy ploys. What was a foregone conclusion is becoming the business scam of the year. A new crop of retail traders was growing, a result of zero-commission, friendly, and intuitive stock trading apps that were increasingly popular among the shelter-in-place status of most people. Gamblers that were accustomed to casinos, the horse track, or betting on professional sports found a new gambling avocation.

During the pandemic, the government was furiously bailing out every troubled company, so somehow the retail trading crowd interpreted that to mean Hertz would be saved. Traders bid up the bankrupt company stock almost a thousand percent in less than two weeks.

Debtor-in-Possession (DIP) financing is the typical means of borrowing money to bridge from bankruptcy to liquidation and wrapping things up. But Hertz, creatively, cleverly, saw the crazy stock action and announced a secondary stock offering, arguing they could avoid the interest expense of a loan and save a lot of money. The Securities and Exchange (SEC) filing was ostensibly approved by the Hertz Board of Directors, the Chief Executive Officer, the Chief Financial Officer, and their auditors.

Days before the stock offering was consummated, the SEC pulled the plug, essentially said, "no." No fines, no penalties, nor admonishment even, just "no." The reason this fraudulent plan was not punished was because in the fine print of the prospectus was a warning that investors were "likely to lose all their money." Retail traders—for the most part—don't read SEC filings so they were queuing up to buy the stock. The proceeds would have

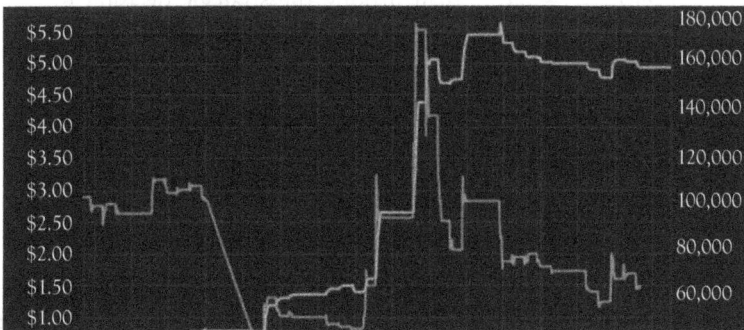

Figure 4.3 Hertz stock

only gone toward senior creditors who would still only recover pennies on the dollar.

Boeing

The Boeing Company designs, manufactures, and sells airplanes, as well as satellites and telecommunications worldwide. Boeing is one of the largest global aerospace manufacturers and the second largest defense contractor. Boeing was a jewel and an icon of American business since 1916. In 2019, Boeing reported $76.6 billion in sales and was ranked 40th among the "Fortune 500" list.

In 2019, Boeing suffered after the 737 MAX was grounded worldwide, a result of two fatal crashes, one in late 2018 and one in early 2019. A long list of strategic blunders has tainted a once great example of American knowhow and success. December 2011 Public Campaign criticized Boeing for spending $52 million lobbying avoiding taxes from 2008 through 2010, instead pocketing $178 million worth of tax rebates. All this in spite of making $9.7 billion in profit. Boeing laid off 14,862 workers since 2008, while increasing executive pay 31 percent to $42 million in 2010 to keep and delight its top five executives.[2] The firm has been criticized for profiting from wars such as the war in Yemen. Its missiles were found used for indiscriminate attacks that resulted in the killing many civilians.

More recently, the 737-Max debacle demonstrated the foolishness of cutting corners on quality. Most of the orders for the plane have since been canceled, yet—rather than making the strategic decision to stop throwing good money after bad—Boeing continues to fight to keep the platform alive.

Finally, in 2020, as a result of the hard-hitting pandemic, Boeing needs money and is looking for governmental help. They should instead consider clawing back the ill-gotten gains of the C-Suite, where executives received lucrative amounts from stock options as company stock purchases sent the prices soaring. Boeing initiated the share purchase program in 2013. Since then, it repurchased $43 billion in common stock. Boeing and other major U.S. airlines, having frittered away $90 billion buying their own shares through the past decade, today need a government bailout, perhaps as much as $110 billion to survive the pandemic-induced recession.

Wells Fargo

In 2015, Wells Fargo grew to become the world's largest bank in terms of market capitalization. Then a scandal broke, involving the creation of over 2 million fake bank accounts, along with illegal manipulation of other accounts by the Wells Fargo employees. In early 2018, the Federal Reserve barred Wells Fargo from growing further its nearly $2 trillion asset base, based upon years of misconduct, requiring Wells Fargo to first fix the internal problems to their satisfaction. In April 2018, The Wall Street Journal reported that the U.S. Department of Labor launched a probe seeking to learn if Wells Fargo was pushing its customers into more expensive retirement plans, including Wells Fargo retirement plans. By May 2018, The Wall Street Journal reported that Wells Fargo's business banking group improperly changed documents dealing with business clients in 2017 and 2018.[3]

The long list of frauds and defalcations has so tarnished the Well Fargo name that the company is struggling, and their stock keeps on falling. Following is a list of the woes that earned this bank a well-deserved moniker: *culture of corruption*.[4]

1. 1981 MAPS Wells Fargo embezzlement scandal
2. Higher costs charged to African American and Hispanic borrowers
3. Failure to monitor suspected money laundering
4. Overdraft fees "gouging"
5. Settlement and fines regarding mortgage servicing practices
6. SEC fine due to inadequate risk disclosures
7. Lawsuit by FHA over loan underwriting
8. Lawsuit due to premium inflation on forced place insurance
9. Lawsuit regarding excessive overdraft fees
10. 2015 Violation of New York credit card laws
11. Executive compensation excesses
12. Tax avoidance and lobbying
13. Prison industry investment

14. SEC settlement for insider trading case
15. Wells Fargo fake accounts scandal
16. Racketeering lawsuit for mortgage appraisal overcharges
17. Dakota Access Pipeline investment
18. Failure to comply with document security requirements
19. Connections to the gun industry and NRA
20. Discrimination against female workers

Summary

The aforementioned three cases are not exceptional, but indeed have become the rule, the norm. As fraudulent practices become mainstream du jour, principled and honest companies are at a competitive disadvantage, leading these upstanding firms to adopt sketchy practices or begin to shrink in terms of their presence.

When it comes to running your business, the two most important focus areas today are: (1) How you treat your employees, and (2) What is your culture, a culture of vice, or a culture of corruption? For there are millions on social media just waiting to pounce if you are not careful, thinking you can hide from them. Finding the *edge of the table*, working the *gray areas*, and *pushing the envelope* are all—in the end—going to finish you off as a going concern.

CHAPTER 5

Trending Businesses

Technology is changing the job landscape faster than ever. If we would draw an axis and place structured jobs on the left axis and highly ambiguous jobs on the right, we can be certain that many of those jobs that would be closer to the left will disappear within a decade, while the emerging jobs on the right will pay for more.

In this chapter, we will cover the areas prone to the greatest amount of change and the opportunities that the changes will provide in terms of employment and businesses.

- Artificial intelligence, machine learning and deep learning
- Edge-computing
- Autonomous vehicles
- 5G
- Finance as it continues to decentralize
- Retail technology
- Smart Home: Software is the new hardware
- Gigs, side hustles, and freelance (covered in Chapters 1 and 2)
- E-commerce
- Going green

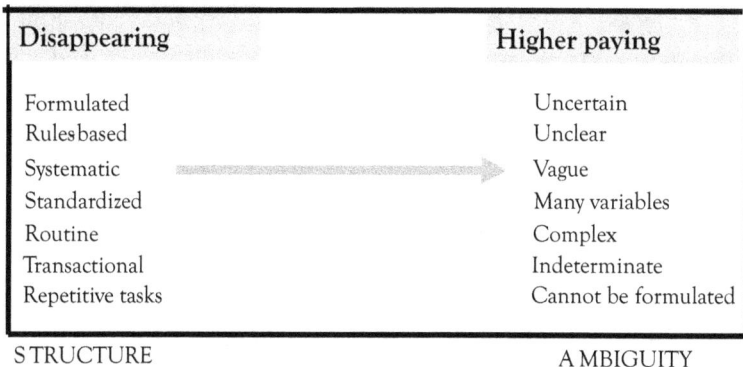

Disappearing	Higher paying
Formulated	Uncertain
Rules based	Unclear
Systematic	Vague
Standardized	Many variables
Routine	Complex
Transactional	Indeterminate
Repetitive tasks	Cannot be formulated

STRUCTURE   AMBIGUITY

Figure 5.1 From "disappearing" jobs to "higher paying jobs"

The purpose of this chapter is to highlight some of the new technologies and trends for those considering new businesses or seeking education and training for jobs within these new businesses. Don't be alarmed by the vernacular, most people will struggle with the terminology because it is in fact bleeding edge high tech with all the science that is moving from the theoretical into the practical realm of products and exciting new benefits and advantages that go with the new product.

In today's environment of uncertainty, it takes serious determination and willpower to pick yourself up by the scruff of the neck and put one foot in front of the other as you make your way into the new jobs the 2020s will be opening up and indeed are opening up already. I am convinced some or even several of these areas will pique your interest and result in either your education and training for work in the new business or even starting a business of your own that is in an area ripe for blossoming and growing.

Artificial Intelligence and Machine Learning

"Artificial intelligence" or AI is a broad term that refers to computer software, which engages seemingly humanlike activities such as learning, problem-solving and planning. AI is already here and everywhere. If you use Alexa, you are using AI. The applications are limitless, impacting every digital market: cybersecurity, healthcare. According to LinkedIn, AI specialist positions were the fastest-growing job titles in 2020.

Some of the applications of AI include chatbots, smart assistants, and self-driving cars. Forward-looking entrepreneurs and executives need to be thinking about ways AI will change their industry and their business within the industry. If you ignore AI, it will come to disrupt you and your business in the not-too-distant future.

Machine learning is a type of artificial intelligence developed for business purposes. Machine learning can be used to process large amounts of data—very fast. This type of artificial intelligence relies upon and utilizes algorithms that "learn" and get better as they get more practice. The more data you can feed a machine learning algorithm, the better the output model becomes, increasing value and usefulness. Think of machine learning as the process of dumping vast troves of data and getting out of it important information for decision making.

Deep learning is an even more specific version of machine learning that relies on neural networks to engage in nonlinear reasoning. Deep learning is critical to performing more advanced functions, such as fraud detection. It can do this by analyzing a wide range of factors at once. For example, for self-driving cars to work, several factors must be identified, analyzed, and responded to at once. Deep learning algorithms are used to help self-driving cars contextualize information picked up by their sensors, like the distance of other objects, the speed at which they are moving and a prediction of where they will be in 5 to 10 seconds. All this information is calculated side by side to help a self-driving car make decisions like when to change lanes.

Deep learning is a part of machine learning, a branch of AI that configures computers to execute tasks through experience. Deep learning models are becoming more and more independent in their own rite, continuing to improve their performance as more data is received. Deep learning models are scalable and detailed. Deep learning has become indispensable in terms of visual art processing, natural language processing, drug discovery and toxicology, customer relationship management, recommendation systems, bioinformatics, medical image analysis, mobile advertising, image restoration, financial fraud detection, and even robot training in the military (through observation).

Edge Computing

The objective of Edge Computing is to take the computation from data centers and move it closer to the edge of the network, exploiting mobile phones or network gateways in order to perform tasks, and provide services on behalf of the cloud. Moving these services to the edge makes it possible to provide content caching, storage, service delivery, and IoT management. This results in improved response times and transfer rates. Privacy and security, scalability, reliability, speed, and efficiency are all markedly improved.

For individuals and businesses that have an interest in this emerging technology, here are just a few places where it is going:

- Big Data Analytics—the utilization of data makes edge computing an ideal candidate to take advantage of technologies such as the Internet of Things (IoT).

- Operational Efficiency—Edge computing systems not only enhance our understanding of customer experiences; retailers rely on the edge computing infrastructure to offer them insights into how to leverage technological resources in order to promote better operational efficiency.
- Custom-made Customer Experiences—Expansion of the IoT along with the increasing connectivity throughout systems and technologies, enabled many new ways to connect and to engage with customers
- Consumer Trends—The understanding of consumer behaviors is enhanced by edge computing, enabling retailers to accumulate insights into just how shoppers behave, in-store and online, through the data collected.
- Security and Surveillance—The IoT with edge computing infrastructure doesn't just allow retailers to comprehend what their data is telling them, in order to improve customer experiences and operational efficiency. New security and surveillance technologies also take advantage of edge computing systems by providing improved security abilities and surveillance features through hardware, cameras, and motion sensors.

Autonomous Vehicles

Developing a driverless car is a hot pursuit and most people recognize the names of the companies and their credibility to deliver this new platform in due course: Google, Tesla, Apple, Lyft, and Uber.

The advantages and benefits these will provide are lower overall costs, better fuel consumption, reduced CO_2 emissions and less congestion on the roads. Well over 90 percent of road accidents are tied to human error, so safety and saving lives is also a major advantage.

Autonomous Vehicle Outlook, written by Allied Market Research, predicts the autonomous vehicle will reach almost $600 billion by 2026, and be growing at almost 40 percent per year through 2026.[1] This nascent business still has to overcome fearful perceptions in the public mind about driverless vehicles. As with any disruptive innovation and iconoclastic invention, the views and attitudes of the people are paramount and can hinder the adoption process and put up many obstacles that must be overcome. Currently, the majority of people have only reached the point of comfort with a driver that is assisted with driving software.

Tesla was the forerunner, the first starter in the electric vehicle space. Today, more than a dozen auto manufacturers are rolling out their own clean energy cars. Likewise, Tesla is ahead in terms of the new driverless technology, but Ford and Volkswagen have created a joint venture to share technology and intellectual property that will be the foundation of their own driverless vehicles. Alphabet/Google started a subsidiary called Waymo. Waymo is pursuing driverless technology for commercial ride-hailing service similar to Uber and Lyft. The size of these tech behemoths and the billions being poured into the driverless dream is daunting. Finding a place for you in this may be frightening since all of it seems well outside of your current job grade. Read about the path and progress and watch for the specifics of positions that are opening already today. As mentioned earlier in the book, these are the companies that will take you right off the street and train and educate you.

5G

The driverless technology previously discussed ties into 5G nicely. Cars will "talk" to each other, warning of road dangers using 5G technology in future. The experts at Glasgow Caledonian University (GCU) are working to enable 5G with driverless cars to send messages about risks such as road work, potholes, ice, or a wreck ahead. The GCU smart connectivity and sensing group uses mobile networks spans that include street-lighting systems, communication, vehicles, and smart cities.[2]

5G is the latest wireless broadband technology; the next generation follows 4G LTE that 98 percent of Americans are currently using. It has the potential to provide speeds as fast as one gigabyte every second. That means, it will be 500 times faster than LTE rate. This high rate would allow the download of an entire HD movie in seconds compared to an hour it takes to do this with its predecessor LTE. It is targeted at the proliferation of devices that need broadband Internet.

Taiwanese semiconductor company MediaTek may not ring a bell but there is a very good chance their chips reside in a product that you own. These semiconductors are found in Amazon Echo, most of smart televisions, even the new Peloton exercise bike. Smartphones, Chromebooks, and many connected products include a MediaTek chip. More recently, MediaTek has embarked on an ambitious 5G development project. The new Dimensity 1000 5G system-on-a-chip (SoC), integrated into the Sub-6 5G modems, boasts significant power efficiency and advanced Wi-Fi 6. For smartphones, Dimensity 1000 5G powers the LG Velvet 5G phone that T-Mobile recently began offering.[3]

Over a hundred thousand new jobs have already been created from 5G technologies in the 12 months through May 2020. By 2034, 5G technologies will have created almost 5 million jobs in metro areas throughout the United States, according to Morning Consult.[4] The report describes how this new generation of wireless technologies will help the U.S. economy. Government agencies such as the Bureau of Labor Statistics (BLS) lack the ability to measure jobs across sectors arising from new technology such as 5G. New jobs in the projections include robotics maintenance, smart grid analysis, telehealth installer, even a tower climber assisting in the 5G buildouts.

My own background includes accounting and finance, and during my career, the field changed considerably. It became highly specialized with arcane terminology and Certified Public Accountants (CPA's) and

Figure 5.2 (DeFi) or Decentralized Finance

Vice Presidents of Finance, both apply to my own career background, commanded high compensation, and were always in high demand in all the medium and large-sized firms. Finance, investing, and banking are all undergoing a sea change of rapidly accelerating new technologies, processes, and services enabled by many of the newly trending technologies, some of which are discussed earlier, such as 5G. These fields continue to evolve, and the migration trends will be identified here for you.

The existing banking and financial systems have relied upon a number of large, highly capitalized financial institutions, regulatory bodies, and law firms that serve as kind of "layer of trust." This sector comprises $4 trillion of our nation's $20 trillion annual GDP, presenting significant systemic risk. In support are many intermediaries: payment service providers (PSP's), third party administrators (TPA's) dedicated to asset management, trade clearinghouses, claims adjustors, and insurance brokers.

This structure began before the Industrial Revolution and evolved to the present-day Information Age. It has weathered booms and busts, periods of growth and recessions, inflation, and changes to the value of the fiat currency. Though we cannot claim stellar execution and consistent stability, the system has largely worked well and served the needs of the nations.

Though 3 out of 4 Americans have less than $2,000 in savings, the industry racks up billions in fees: overdraft fees, nonsufficient funds fees, transaction and commission fees, and many more. It is estimated that $350 billion goes to administration costs, insurance brokers, and corporate profits, and all of this presents an opportunity to attack and reduce some of what could essentially be termed, from the consumer perspective, "waste costs."

DeFi is gaining in popularity, particularly when the global economic outlook has deteriorated as a result of the COVID-19 pandemic. Traditional financial institutions have failed to uphold the interests of people, and the shot-gunning of monetary and fiscal stimulus has helped a bit, but it has also been problematic as it was far too hurried and generalized, not the least bit carefully planned, thought out, and managed. Even dead people received their stimulus checks.

The concept of blockchain-based DeFi is today gaining traction as it allows individuals or companies to create financial applications sans the usual third-party intermediaries. DeFi applications are built on the blockchain network, the foundation that underpins Bitcoin today, using a protocol specific to the network. The purpose of DeFi is to take traditional financial services directly to everyone using the blockchain infrastructure. DeFi is "An ecosystem of applications built on public distributed ledgers, to facilitate permission-fewer financial services."

DeFi offers the promise of creating a robust financial market, decentralizing financial activities such as trading, lending, investment, wealth management, insurance, and cross-border payments through the use of the blockchain technology

DeFi relies on decentralized application (DApps), making use of DApps protocols, along with smart contract features operating as integrate connectors that enable a peer-to-peer financial network. DeFi can be implemented with the blockchain protocols, yet Ethereum is growing in the DeFi activity space because it is a very popular platform in which developers create their own unique DApps. Other platforms (EOS, NEO, and more) are attempting to offer more developer-related options and alternatives in order to gain traction. Yet, given that cross-chain compatibility continues as a primary issue, early adopters of Ethereum blockchain remain.

What can be expected in terms of jobs, careers, and new businesses in DeFi? You are working today as a lawyer, but this pandemic and recession has resulted in fewer clients and falling revenue. Why not consider a logical next step in your career? Smart contracts. A smart contract is a protocol for parties to deal directly with each other without the need for a third-party, the lawyer has been removed from the equation. Ethereum capitalized on smart contracts as the starter in the development of the first DApps development platform. Since that time, it became the blockchain of choice for companies that wanted to create their financial products. Today a majority of DeFi applications are built on Ethereum, the most innovation can be found on their blockchain.

Besides smart contracts, the opportunities span a wide variety of possibilities in companies such as Compound Finance, dYdX, Set Protocol, Dharma, Uniswap, Maker, Aave, and PoolTogether[5]:

- Ethereum engineer
- Back-end developer

- QA tester
- DevOps engineer
- Scrum master
- Software engineer
- Product design
- Business ops and strategy
- Contract engineer

Retail Technology

Earlier, we discussed the Internet of Things (IoT). IoT and smart equipment are already moving heavily into the retail space with sensor-embedded shelves to track inventory and personalized shopping experiences for consumers. Messaging-based customer service (chat) bots have been testing across at least half of the Fortune 5000. Artificial intelligence bots improve customer experiences and robotic store assistants are asking and answering consumer questions.

When it comes to stock management, automating the warehouse has vastly improved inventory control. Having accurate counts and changes to counts help with forecasting replenishment, assessing high and low demand inventory and avoiding waste costs like spoilage and product obsolescence. Inventory turns can be improved, consequently, reducing the need for excess warehouse space.

The "Amazon Effect" means, in order to survive, companies must strive to adopt and utilize some of the best practices in terms of technology found at Amazon today. In just a few years, it is expected that over a half million autonomous mobile robots (AMR) will be assisting warehouses in the fulfillment of their orders. Order times and processing times will drop significantly, as will the need for human laborers.

Facial recognition software can help catch the bad guys as well as cater to the good customers, but a lot of privacy concerns limit the use of this technology. Facial recognition technology is biometric, meaning it applies statistical data to biological data. Other types of biometrics are voice recognition, retina scanning and fingerprint matching. In the United States, the Fifth Amendment protects citizens from having to give up potentially incriminating information about themselves. While a business may want to identify those with extremist political or religious ideologies if biometrics can help them to do so, or those with a criminal background, rights and protections will not want to allow that type of technology to be used.

We are followed around as a result of our online browsing habits. Ever notice that after you searched for an umbrella that a lot of subsequent sites you later frequented had tiny ads on the sides for umbrellas, and maybe raincoats and boots? This is part and parcel to predictive analytics that Amazon, Shopify, and Netflix currently employ. It can be annoying, but it can also result in you purchasing an item recommended to you that you never thought of before. *Recommendation engines* are powerful predictive retail tools that direct and funnel purchasing options to consumers at the optimal times.

Today's sales associates with customer service chops are using their mobile apps with retail settings that must be developed and must be deployed. Stores need employees comfortable with these tools. Employees need to be trained that today's shoppers are completely different than shoppers of just a couple years ago, but at the same time they need to be able to cater to the consumer that is not tech savvy, for both types matter to the retail business. Customer service remains the number one skill needed in retail. Customers demand great service no matter how they are shopping, and the challenge to employees is they are less and less patient.

Chief customer office positions are in high demand. These people have enterprisewide responsibility for everything from strategy, processes, and technology to sensing the changing needs and demands of consumers. Techie-types too are highly valued in this space. IT professionals, software developers, and those internet-savvy are in high demand in retailing as is the use of social media. Finally, the big data crunchers—customer analytics—covers all the areas of marketing, technology, and social media to extract information from the data.

Smart Home: Software Is the New Hardware

We begin with a list of some of the top home automation systems:

- Amazon Echo
- Google Nest Hub

- Wink Hub 2
- Samsung SmartThings
- Apple HomeKit

Wireless technology and connectivity mean more opportunities to automate and control lighting, heating, and entertainment centers with little more than a visual interface, your mobile phone or even your voice. For only one to two hundred dollars, a homeowner can enable a video doorbell, arm home security, ensure the temperature in the house is what you want it to be when you want it. There are also smart plugs and lights, along with the smoke and detectors, even the door locks of your home. Beyond this, we have smart televisions, music systems, and audio-visual entertainment. Robots ready to vacuum floors or mow the grass. Smart wireless technology controls it all.

Home builders are not typically associated with new technologies in the homes they design and build. But a need exists for smart-home savvy people as the means of introducing not just smart home products and services, but solar and other new technologies to bring to home buyers. Amazon, Cox, and Comcast are also trying to become a part of this new channel.

Builders across the country are training in these technologies to upgrade understanding and tech-based skills that are coming to be expected in new home subdivisions. While solar is a tough sell to a homeowner with clay tile roof that is just fine, and unsure if he will still have that home in five years, new homes can roll into the mortgage the cost of all these new technologies with a compelling cost-benefit sales pitch.

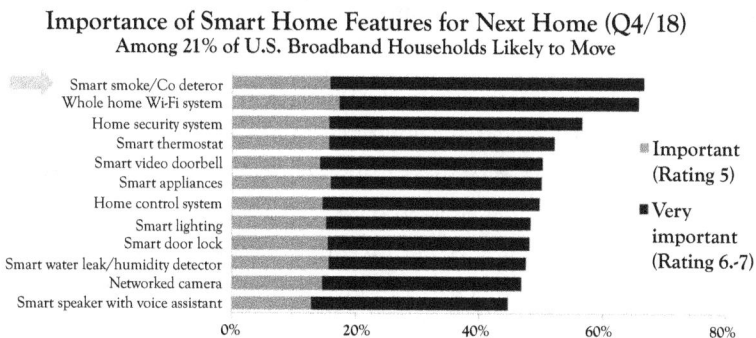

Importance of Smart Home Features for Next Home (Q4/18)
Among 21% of U.S. Broadband Households Likely to Move

Figure 5.3 Smart home features[6]

Drivers, customer service, sales reps, remote data entry, call center, and smart-home product techs are just a few of the new jobs this technology has already created. The best business opportunity is to create a new business that is the channel or intermediary between the tech products and their companies, and the sales outlets. The sales side consists of home builders, kiosks in places like Lowe's or Home Depot, retail stores, and online shopping businesses.

E-Commerce Dominates

The leveraging of e-mail will continue to grow with companies like Rebel developing the means for e-commerce brands to sell through e-mail. Combining all social networks in terms of the revenue they drive, e-mail is greater than them all with its ability to drive customers directly to a specific website.

The opportunities in this space are for those in PR, or search, or digital. To develop the means to make the lives of customers easier while building trust. Your e-commerce goals will include a laser focus on the continuation of customer engagement through the favorable experiences they have enjoyed. The amount of e-commerce advertising will continue to grow and create brands for businesses that can engage customers well beyond just the purchase function. If you lose a customer, the cost of getting that customer back puts you at a distinct competitive disadvantage.

The majority of customers do some amount of research prior to making their purchase. This means that their search results must take them to your content and that content must be trusted. Align that content with your strategy, and the strategy should make sense in terms of the market you seek to attract, the demographic, the type of customer, all of what best characterizes who your intended customers are.

Your brand needs to have an almost anthropomorphic vibe, meaning it should have a personality that is humanizing and evokes a sense of pleasantness, even joy. That, at least, is the goal, for you need as many differentiating factors as you can come up with. Coca Cola, Disney, Siri, and Budweiser are all brands that have captured the joy of their customers and have kept the customers from wandering off to other brands. Technology provides the capability of creating personalization, particularly in terms of the customer online experience.

We are now witnessing the advent and acceleration of voice search. Most of the searches will be done via voice within just a few years, along with interactive content, mobile optimization, and video, as user interface and experiences are steadily improving and getting better all the time. E-commerce trends mean more e-commerce businesses and more e-commerce related jobs. That may be the most interesting and attractive area that draws you in.

CHAPTER 6

Manufacturing Businesses

This chapter begins, rather than ends, with a case study. It is drawn from my own experience and career because it touched on most of what it takes to be successful in manufacturing. Though this was some time back, the basics and concepts remain relevant to this day. My journey began as vice-president of manufacturing operations for Seagate Technology, building drives that store digital data.

When I was promoted to run the global manufacturing for Seagate, we had this profile:

- Drive factory in Singapore
- Head engineering in California, manufacturing in Malaysia
- Packout operations in California
- Sales and service in the United States, Europe, and Asia

We were doing okay, but just okay. I hired a very capable general manager in Singapore and contracted with Pittiglio-Rabin-Todd-McGrath (now PwC) for manufacturing operations consulting. The goal was to completely, top-to-bottom revolutionize our manufacturing operations.

Defective part per million (DPPM) was a target, it was too high as were other inefficiencies and waste costs. We had a lot of rework, needed a second shift that required shift premium, suffered scrap and yield losses, and our inventory was turning over so slowly that shrinkage, excess inventory, and obsolescence plagued our overall manufacturing cost.

We built our drives to finished goods based upon workorders that we pulled each day. We staged the parts and subassemblies on the factory floor, and more often than not, came up short on parts that we then expedited so we could complete the workorder. We had far too many SKU's (stock keeping units), both in raw drive configurations and finished goods, so much like a car dealer's lot, we had tons of product that mostly no one demanded.

First up, we re-engineered the drive. This of course necessitated the involvement of both design and manufacturing engineering. The goal was to create a "postponement model" for the drive. What that means is our Singapore factory would build a plain vanilla, generic drive that would wait to be "flavored" until it reached the pack out locations in the United States, Europe, and Asia.

We then abandoned workorders altogether and set up flowlines with Kanbans behind each worker that held their components for assembling and packing out the drives. We tasked our suppliers with keeping tabs on the raw material. Sometimes the variability required they visit every day to ensure no stock out and replenishment was limited to the number of containers that fit behind each worker. At the front-end of each flowline were Kanban squares that our Singapore factory was charged with keeping replenished with generic, plain vanilla drives. Don't run out, but don't exceed the space you have been allocated.

We changed the model from "build to finished goods" to "build to demand," although "demand" included 4-weeks inventory in the hands of our distributors. If there was no demand there was no manufacturing activity, we never built just to keep workers busy doing things to earn their pay. The lines were balanced as industrial engineers determined what each worker would be doing as they pulled generic drives and moved them down the lines to add bezels, software, accessories, and packaging that aligned with the day's demand.

The results were incredible:

- Elimination of finished goods freeing up factory floor space
- Elimination of second shift even as shipment volumes were growing
- Elimination of excess and obsolete inventory
- Reduction of waste costs (more on that later—Six Sigma projects)
- Much higher customer fulfillment in much shorter fulfillment times
- Higher gross profits as manufacturing drive costs were reduced

In parallel with our consultants and the re-engineering of our manufacturing operations, we took advantage of Seagate's new initiative, a $10 million investment in Six Sigma. I and several others studied at Scottsdale's Six Sigma Academy and immersed ourselves in manufacturing improvement projects. One of those projects tackled our manufacturing bottleneck. It was in the Singapore factory final test. The test took too long and the number of expensive testers too few.

A bright young Master Blackbelt rewrote the test software based upon a pareto of typical errors the test would sometimes find. The test was now first looking for the most common error or defect, and after this the second most common, and so forth. Given probability and statistical mathematics, we found we could cut the last part of the test entirely, reducing the test time by almost 50 percent and doubling our throughput. Altogether, our Six Sigma projects reduced DPPM from 40 k to around 5 sigma (233 defective parts per million), scrap, rework, and other waste costs were moving steadily toward zero, and as a result, waste costs that had been attacked with a vengeance had become miniscule.

Costs can be stratified into three broad categories, each having an entirely different goal and objective:

1. *Value-add costs.* These are labor and variable overhead that improves the value of the product that will be sold. Besides value-add manufacturing, you can also include sales calls, customer service, direct marketing, design engineering, and similar efforts that are part and parcel to enhancing revenue and profitability.

2. *Nonvalue-add costs.* These are unavoidable costs that nevertheless should be kept to a minimum. Costs such as compliance, accounting, IT, security, utilities, regulatory reporting, some of the marketing that does not lend itself to the direct measurement of the sales, executive, and managerial hierarchies that are mostly oversight in nature, and noncritical travel. This is a category that although the costs are unavoidable, the goal is to minimize them.

3. *Waste costs.* These are the costs a company would like to drive to zero. They include such things as scrap, rework, retesting, reanything, shift premiums, parts expediting, overtime, inventory shrinkage and obsolescence, and the cost of all inefficiencies.

Warren Buffett once famously said, "when the tide goes out you see who was swimming naked." Likewise, when a recession hits, you see who was financially unprepared, in terms of government, business, education, and households. The pandemic collapsed the economy and along with high unemployment demand cratered. This led many companies to beg government for bailouts. The CARES Act was intended to direct trillions in liquidity to bridge us from the onset of the pandemic to what we thought would eventually be a return to pre-pandemic prosperity. But as this virus hangs on more and more, companies are unable to hang on. Although the liquidity provided by the government was a lifesaver, the longer-term problem now is companies faced with insolvency.

Fixed Costs => Sticky Costs

To survive, companies in many cases need to lower their breakeven points. But to so, they need to shed fixed assets. Either they sell assets such as excess factory capacity, machinery and equipment or buildings, or they simply shutter these so there is no longer ongoing support and maintenance costs. Fixed costs are also called "sticky cost," for good reason. Unlike variable costs that can be relatively ratcheted up and down as required, fixed cost like property, plant, and equipment are not so easily dispositioned.

Tesla has been in business for 17 years. They chose the path of owning and financing their own factories. Recently, they chose to move out of the factory in Fremont, California and fire up a new factory in Austin, Texas. They opened a factory in Shanghai, China, and a new factory to build their much-acclaimed Cybertruck will soon open in Germany. That has resulted in a challenge when it comes to profitability, for these factories need to be operating at 80 percent capacity or higher to spread unit fixed costs over as many vehicles as possible.

Two things Elon Musk, the CEO of Tesla, neglected to consider in terms of the high costs of factories that manufacture cars:

- The recession resulting from the pandemic would reduce capacity utilization rates in the factories, increasing fixed costs per unit on a declining volume.

- Dozens of competitors would finally tool-up to compete with Tesla in the EV space.

If it wasn't for the EV credits granted to Tesla from the government, the company would have never made a dime, after almost two decades of trying. And the future is looking challenging, as JD Powers ranks their quality low and competitive models are getting high marks. The cult of Tesla worshippers who as at this writing bid Tesla's stock price up ten times what it was a year ago, making it the world's most valuable automotive company, are in for a bitter surprise.

What is the lesson learned? When you are new in a business you seek flexibility, not low unit costs, for you don't know with assurance that you will achieve and sustain high enough volumes to remain profitable and generate sufficient cash flow to avoid insolvency, bankruptcy. Large semiconductor fabs now require billions and billions to build. Companies that need semiconductors are moving toward a fab-less model, concerning themselves only with the design, form, fit, function, then sending the design out to subcontract manufacturers.

Likewise, your own manufacturing requirements could mostly—at least initially—be outsourced. In addition, you can outsource many other functions such as IT, accounting, taxes, even HR and payroll. Only as your company grows, and you can demonstrate that you have a compelling cost and strategic reason to bring one or more of these functions in-house, should you consider doing so.

Manufacturing Trends

Reshoring. With the administration of President Trump, there has been a strong move to bring manufacturing back home to the United States, both from consumers and business. The offshoring movement in search of cheap labor began in the 1970's. But the labor that seemed cheap offshore is in many cases more expensive today when you consider administrative costs, shipping costs, and increasing labor costs. Unskilled manufacturing labor, along with the related overhead, is no longer cheaper by any measure in places like Taiwan and Shanghai. Meanwhile, the lack of upward progress in the U.S. wages has changed the calculus significantly.

Here is a list of some of the perceived benefits of reshoring:

1. U.S. unemployment is high in the pandemic-induced recession
2. Logistics and distribution technology and processes have become one of America's competitive advantages (consider Amazon)
3. A U.S. company with a U.S. plant has more control over manufacturing cost, quality, and output here versus offshore
4. What is learned in the production process adds to the knowledge base and the ability to continue to improve and progress more in the future
5. Quality control is assured when you have local control; it can become problematic in the hands of a subcontract manufacturer oceans away

Green Manufacturing. Green manufacturing and sustainability initiative are in vogue. Less waste, less energy, reduced carbon footprint, are giving rise to the following trends:

1. Converting raw material into finished product necessitates the consumption of energy. Renewable energy is what progressive companies are striving to adopt, both as a potential cost reduction goal and to be seen as being concerned about corporate social responsibility. Solar and other renewables will continue to grow as fossil fuel-based energy demand wanes.
2. Waste destined for landfills contributes to environmental degradation, so sustainable disposal methods are replacing dumping. Manufactures are reducing emissions and changing to recycling and reusing to reduce waste. Today, tech firms like Apple and Dell will give you credit for your new purchase when you trade in your old monitor, printer, or computer so they can safely dispose of it. Also, you may be focused on manufacturing recyclable plastics and metals. Within a few years, the additive manufacturing market is expected to grow to $50 billion.
3. 3D Printing and Additive Manufacturing are beneficial in terms of flexible manufacturing and digital efficiencies. In the case of

3D printing, you may drastically reduce parts' transportation costs and wasted material. 3-D printing processes include:

a. Material extrusion

b. Material jetting

c. Directed energy

d. Deposition Powder

e. Sheet lamination

f. Binder jetting

4. Green cars. We wrote earlier about the fact that Tesla was the lead manufacturer of electric vehicles, and how today many other companies are competing with them to develop environmentally friendly cars. Honda has invested a considerable sum to produce fuel-efficient vehicles and seeks to come out with vehicles powered by hydrogen. Prius came out with the world's first hybrid to reach mass market; today, people in over 38 countries are buying it. All this is intended to decrease carbon emissions and improve fuel consumption.

5. Water conservation. Water is an essential commodity, as the world increasingly needs more water, it needs more energy. Manufacturing processes use water and conservation is becoming paramount. Clean drinking water, efficient agriculture, and the use of water in production are all leading to novel methods to minimize the consumption of water.

6. Packaging sustainability. Consumers are cutting down on the need for so much plastic. Likewise, manufacturers' packaging methods are changing. Collapsible bulk boxes, reusable packaging, the ability to reuse boxes can eliminate the need to continuously buy and assemble new boxes in each shipment.

Manufacturers, along with their supply chains are working to improve risk management. Risk management strategies will encompass internal operations in terms of how operations impact the supply chain. The factors under review include the environment and the impact upon consumer health. This entails finding a trade-off and a balance instead of simply maximizing profit.

Collaboration is another focus area in future manufacturing. 3PL partnerships are being formed for the purpose of exchanging information between the purchasing function and the manufacturing function in the hopes of reducing cost and errors, increasing productivity, and improving efficiency.

Regulatory changes are coming fast and furious, many simplified and negated entirely by the Trump Administration; manufacturers now have much greater freedom to pursue new products as well as the means of manufacturing. Yet manufacturers still must take all steps and ensure safeguards are in place, so the public does not view the firm adversely. Continued investments in research and development will go hand-in-hand with the expansion of current products; for consumers, hunger for the latest and greatest technology, product, as manufacturers who are not changing and moving forward will quickly lose the demand they once enjoyed.

New manufacturing strategies are being developed that pivot from increased knowledge of what consumers demand. Expect an increase in 3PL outsourcing of transportation and services. This will reduce cost as low cost 3PL providers can perform these services cheaper, faster and more efficiently.

Finally, we are seeing more "outcome-based pricing" among manufacturers, particularly in the pharmaceutical and medical supply chain. This is a relatively new adoption and a narrow application at this date, but we can expect more adoption in the years to come.

CHAPTER 7

Service Businesses

The bad news is that as this pandemic has ravaged customer-facing businesses such as cruise lines, airlines, movie theaters, salons, entertainment venues, professional sports, and restaurants, a great many businesses have shuttered permanently and filed for bankruptcy. The silver lining in the Covid cloud is that coming out of the pandemic would be an excellent time to open your own service business, as competition will be far lower, and demand will be high. The year 2021 will be opportunistic for those with creative ideas for their intended customer-facing business, a chance to bring to the new business the most up-to-date thinking in terms of what Millennials and Gen-Z enjoy, as those generations going forward will be the majority of your business.

Amazon and DoorDash are just two of the many companies that adapted to the pandemic to accommodate service needs that used to be fulfilled in retail outlets. But coming out of the pandemic, with far fewer retail outlets, timing would be critical making your new retail presence a big hit. Accenture predicts that Millennials now account for almost $1.4 trillion in spending.* The spending patterns are quite different from their parents', however. Millennials are far more experience driven. They are looking for experiences through technology, entertainment, and travel in lieu of just buying more stuff such as apparel and home accessories. Customization attracts them and the mainstream business practices and products offered to everyone in the past will never interest this generation.

Millennials and Gen Z are no longer interested in expensive brands or chain coffee shops. Understated is fine, t-shirts and sweats and a good coffee in a shop with ambience and social relevance and relatedness are the appeal today. Consequently, shopping malls, chain restaurants and other retail outlets are all going the way of the dodo bird. The lack of loyalty is a myth and misplaced label attached to the younger generation. They are quite loyal in fact, but they want to feel welcomed and they want to be treated right, and the services they seek have changed radically over just the past few years. It is a myth that Millennials only want to shop online.

Retailers must place their focus on five key areas today:

- *Consistent experiences*—with customized offerings with the same experience whether a digital device-based transaction or in-store
- *Personalized interaction*—detailed customer information provides the basis for personal, even local interaction. Displays should be interactive, for example, let the customer look at the video or listen to the music they like. Perhaps part of the display allows shoppers to thank pandemic first responders.
- *Connected shopping*—Once again, the e-commerce and in-store experiences should be the same, both, for example, offering the same advertised discount or promotion item. This can only be successfully accomplished by means of a unified functional retail organization, one that integrates very closely the technology, online, in-store, marketing, and sales functions.
- *Integrated merchandising*—Digital tools are making full merchandising-supply chain integration a reality. The old model of independent functional flow and inventory stock decisions, forwarded to logistics and distribution for execution, must be replaced with agile innovation and integration. That means a compressed drawing-board-to-shelf cycle, multichannel ordering, a reliance on external sourcing for experiential shopping offerings, and ever-changing customer demands are pushing their legacy supply systems and processes to the breaking point. Eventually, these pressures could prompt retailers to accept the challenge of merchandising-supply chain integration.
- *Flexible fulfillment alternatives*—FBA (Fulfillment by Amazon). Amazon is the 800-pound gorilla and the standard-bearer when it comes to fulfillment, no doubt about that. There is a sequence of events that happen following every customer purchase, and today, the customer is looking for

next-day or even same day deliver. Very challenging: sales order processing, checkout, payment, inventory, picking, packing, shipping, and delivering. Returns and exchanges mean robust and friendly customer service and support. You can of course use Amazon for your own business, but the top three alternatives that are pretty good rivals include ShipBob, FedEx, and ShipWire. Apart from these four choices, anything else would be risky in this age of advanced logistics, fulfillment, and delivery technologies and processes.

Restaurants

Conventional wisdom claims 90 percent of new restaurants fail in the first year, up to 90 percent. That is simply false. Statistics vary widely but one study puts the failure rate closer to 26 percent fail in the first year.[1] Getting past the first year in business, chances of failure falls dramatically. The study authors point out that if 90 percent of new restaurants failed in the first year, we would see fewer restaurants each year. Meaning the total number of restaurants in existence would drop and within a decade or so, we would have only half the current number of restaurants. The math just doesn't work.

Five fundamentals stand out among all great restaurants. First, friendly and personalized service. Treat your guests as human beings who deserve kindness and good service, not as people to provide food to then move along to make room for the next customers. Beginning with hosts and servers, strive for sincerity and an upbeat nature about you and everyone working in the restaurant; for customer, feel the vibe. That means taking care and caution whom you hire. Your hires must be likable people, plain and simple. They must have a quick cadence without appearing rushed, smile often, be outgoing, and possess the ability to multitask, all while maintaining grace under pressure.

Second, although it may seem like a small thing, if you can address your guest by name, you have already won the battle for their heart with your sincerity and smile. There is a measurable and pleasurable brain response when someone hears their first name spoken. They will like you more and liking you more will result in listening more carefully to server suggestions, such as the best wine to have with your entrée, for example. That is the means by which you will increase both your tip as well as revenue per table.

Third, the food you prepare and serve is the cornerstone of your restaurant business and one of the most important factors when it comes to how guests perceive their restaurant experience. Top notch food quality control as well as very specific and accurate information that your guest may have simply suggested and only anecdotally, when delivered *exactly* how they like it leads to both repeat visits and word of mouth advertising. All the staff, not just cooks, should be empowered to give feedback on food preparation, quality, and customer satisfaction.

Fourth, restaurant ambience and aesthetics matter a great deal. Location, exterior façade, color scheme, furniture, lighting, not necessarily trendy décor but the *right* décor that best suits the demographic target market you seek as your customers. Go for a consistent theme throughout but go especially for authenticity.

Fifth, and finally, efficient customer service matters as much as the prior four factors. Every aspect, in terms of what is happening when the customer comes in and needs to be seated, to ordering, being served, finishing their meal, getting a timely bill, and even helping if the bill will be split. There should be nothing off-putting or leading to customer impatience, everything must be smooth, predictable, and meet or exceed expectations.

That list can be tough and challenging, daunting even, but if you have your strategy in place and communicate it well to every employee, hire very carefully, and treat your workers fairly, you can inculcate a metronome of habits that ensure repeatability and no unpleasant surprises or angry, disgruntled customers who just may go out and skewer you on Yelp.

Salons

Many salons have closed as the pandemic took its toll. Hair salons, nail salons, acupuncture, massage, and physical therapy. For a great long while, the businesses were shuttered. Then many reopened under stringent and limited conditions that included strict social distancing, the wearing of masks, and a limit on the number of clients and customers that could be inside a given establishment.

The same can be said for gyms. Chains have filed for bankruptcy, and as of this writing, some have reopened but under strictly enforced safety and health guidelines. I recently returned to my own gym after staying away more than six months. There is a limit to how much exercise one can do indoors and even outdoors. Leaving the gym, I looked at a long line of masked members waiting their turn to be allowed in. I felt badly for everyone involved, members, businesses, franchises, seemingly everyone has been negatively impacted and we will soon be coming around to a year in this dire condition as the vaccine appears yet a few months off.

But your idea of a salon may be timely, as post-pandemic, the demand for salon services will be met with limited supply and constrained capacity. This is your chance to plan your salon and the time you are opening at or around vaccine deployment. So, what are the critical factors to consider if you want to open a new salon in your area?

Start with what we call a USP (Unique Selling Proposition). What will be different about what you offer in your salon? While it should not be a cookie-cutter salon that looks like most others, be sure to visit some of the more successful salons to get a flavor for their businesses in terms of the ambience, décor, services offered, personalities of the employees, pricing, location, and any other factors you may notice. Unless you are planning to offer something highly specialized, unique, and differentiated from your competition, advertising would mostly be wasted money.

Offering organic salon products is probably one good path. Pointing out that the products are healthy, safe, and environmentally friendly is important to Millennials and Gen Z today. Doing that might imply that your advertising should be done in your local organic newspaper rather than more generalized media. Your advertising should be laser-targeted to your niche audience, the clientele you are seeking to attract and retain.

Your marketing strategy will consist of advertising, promotion, and communication. Advertising initiatives could be placing a print ad in your local organic paper, as we alluded to earlier, or they could be on a billboard, or even part of an ad campaign on your local radio station.

Promotion does not necessarily require paid media, but it must be creative to attract new clients. Examples of promotions: "Bring a Friend" night, a referral program in your salon, employee discount programs for local employers, or as a guest speaker on a radio talk show program locally.

Communications refers to the creation of a clear presence for your new salon. A few examples of communication: attractive signage, press releases about upcoming events, and an intuitive website listed in all of the local directories. A salon is all about image, but that is trite and superficial. Today, consumers are loyal to a salon more in terms of what it represents rather than how it looks. No more rock music, lights, and fancy and expensive hairbrushes. Today you create and build upon not so much *image* as *client affinity*. Client affinity alludes to the development of a feeling of kinship, an almost natural attraction to a particular business, because that, in turn translates into customer loyalty. You build this affinity via a set of shared goals and values, and a consistent theme in terms of mission and culture. This is called your *ethos*. Your clients are most probably attuned to the types of products and services that enhance and improved their health, their well-being, and their social and environmental responsibility and stewardship.

Be smart when it comes to pricing. The adage "you get what you pay for" can result in low prices being construed as service lacking style and panache. Higher prices can imply higher quality service and will also enable you to offer promotions that provide discounts. Some people will shop price and price only, but where salons have successfully differentiated themselves, you will find that that group is not your target market anyway. Client loyalty will mean the tolerance of prices a bit higher than some of your competitors but competing on price only in such a service business means you have to be in a low-rent location, paying low wages to workers and turning over customers at high volume. While that may be exactly the business model some people envision for themselves, it is unlikely to ever be highly profitable.

Customer Service Challenges

We discussed at some length the different ways and means to differentiate your service business that you might open following a pandemic that shuttered a lot of you competitors. We also listed the ways to strengthen and improve your chances for success, what to do right, what to strive to do better, all the things that matter most in a service business. Now we turn to a few negative factors and how to deal with these unfortunate challenges that nevertheless you will encounter in due course.

Yesterday I called customer service at Amazon. I had received a large box containing a lamp shade. On the box it said, "One of two boxes." I wanted to know where my lamp was. After a long while, I disconnected and tried their chat service. It popped up "48 in the queue ahead of you, estimated wait 5 minutes, 36 seconds." I made a little lunch while keeping a watchful eye on the progress of the chat. I watched the queue number steadily go down until it reached zero and a message popped up, "someone will be with you very soon." Another several minutes later I was chatting with Amazon customer service.

A lot of text about hoping I was having a nice day and how she aimed to help resolve my problem. Several times she asked me to wait patiently while she "looked into" the issue. She even texted she was getting another customer service rep on the chat (that never happened though she went quiet for a long time). After a total of about one hour, she said she would have to look into it further with the vendor and that was likely to take a few days. I told her just cancel. She responded that she already told me what she could and would do. Then she asked me if her efforts resolved my problem. I wrote, "you are fortunate I am not a mystery shopper working for your company," and disconnected.

While you don't expect poor customer service with the likes of an Amazon, virtually everyone has a similar story or two of some customer service rep wasting their time and never delivering a solution to the problem. There will be times when the best way to resolve a customer issue is to transfer the customer to some other person. Never make the mistake of doing a "blind transfer," meaning a transfer of the customer to someone else without first verifying that they are available to take the call. This was the mistake my Amazon chat person made.

What if you simply don't have an answer to a question? This challenge is more about what you should not do than what you should do. It is crucial that you avoid being unclear in your response. Best to deal with customers with sincerity, if you simply do not have the answer, acknowledge that, ask for time to find a solution, and guarantee you will be contacting them. Be specific about how you will contact them and when.

Figure 7.1 Customer service—handle with care

Utilize the HEARD approach to help customer: Hear, Empathize, Apologize, Resolve, Diagnose. If you can master this you are likely to calm irate customers and that will give you the time you need to successfully diagnose and solve the problem.

Many customers are simply not doing a very good job at conveying the specific problem they called or chatted about. This can be frustrating for a customer service rep. I had a terrible experience when I moved recently, and my new router was not connecting to my modem and I could not use the new Wi-Fi service. The tech on the phone knew all the jargon, and though my background is a tech career, he lost me many times with his questions and suggestions. We did manage to get through, and at the end, I was sweaty and had a headache, for we had tried virtually every possible combination and permutation before finally achieving success. Take notes when you pick up the call, assume the caller is clueless, not in the sense of looking down at them, but only in the spirit of keeping the conversation free of miscommunication and jargon that you know well but they may not.

Customer service reps are trained to juggle multiple customers. With tricks like "I am going to put you on hold while I check something for you," only to pick up another call, that is a formula for disaster, and you will find that the customer can figure out he or she is being played and angrily hang up. If you are training your customer service reps to handle multiple calls, you are asking for trouble.

I mentioned I had moved recently. Most of the furniture I needed was delivered outside my door on the second floor of a large apartment complex. I received a call on my cell phone from a delivery driver who had my room air conditioner, which of course was quite heavy. I asked him to bring it on up, knowing that he was young and strong in this type of job and surely had a dolly in his truck. His response? "This is curbside only." I tried to convince him to help me, but he finally said to me, apparently exasperated, "so you're refusing delivery?" I said, "no I am refusing your proposal." He drove away and I requested credit of the charge and bought A/C from the competitor.

The first vendor called and asked me why I didn't offer the driver a tip to bring the product up to my apartment. I said that I did not know that was an option, the driver did not give me any hint. Then he asked if I wanted a discount. I told him I already found the product elsewhere. But my point here is to be very careful about offering discounts or gift cards because that can actually be a turn-off in the eyes of the customer and tarnish your brand.

Lastly, every once in a while, you have to fire a customer. That is never easy, obviously. But some people are problematic, requiring far too much maintenance and never seem capable of being satisfied. When you do encounter these people, you need to take some of the blame, admit the fault is with you (even though it may not be), be appreciative that the customer came to you in the first place, apologize, and suggest an alternative. Going above and beyond what you think you owe this malcontented customer could result in you avoiding an adverse post on social media. You want to avoid—to the best of your ability anyway— creating an atmosphere that results in a customer only wanting to seek petty vengeance online.

CHAPTER 8

Decade 2020s and the New Normal

Decade 2020s and New Businesses That Will Emerge

By now, we have all seen drones somewhere at some time. I used to see people in parks with their new drone testing its capabilities in range, speed, turns, and altitude. The drones were being used for picture and video purposes for the most part. Then they were expensive, but today not so much.

AI (artificial intelligence) is impacting many aspects of our lives now, and in due course, connectivity will include its integration throughout most applications we need. Drones today are multipurpose. They can be used for peering into buildings or dropping ordnance on the heads of enemies. They can enter caves, mines, volcanoes, and tunnels to look around on our behalf. But for our purposes, we mention their use with e-commerce. Amazon and others can now deliver packages, as far away as 15 miles in well under an hour transportation time. This logistics model will in time lead the drone to become the dominant delivery choice.

Renewable energy, in the context of the present global concern with climate change, is creating tons of new opportunities in terms of jobs and businesses. The energy potential in a dam is harnessed via photovoltaic power stations. Utility poles are being removed making more space available for other useful development and purposes. Even new hats with solar panels will charge your digital devices as you walk outdoors. The shift out of fossil fuels for energy is well underway and that shift is creating a lot of new opportunities.

Nanotechnology is going to increase our life span. Miniature robots under 100 nanometers are being injected to tackle chronic diseases formerly resistant to anything other than palliative treatment of symptoms. Combine this technological breakthrough with AI and quantum computing and you have fast answers from data-driven diagnoses that will mean healthier, happier lives.

Related to the advent of medical mini-robots is the emerging field of robot repair. Robots are present in industry, especially dominant in high-volume manufacturing and warehousing. Beyond these applications, robots can be valuable assistants in military, schools, and healthcare. Later in the book, we address the replacement of a large swatch of the workforce with robots and what the implications are for this trend.

Learning the skill and trade of robot repair is going to become a big deal in the future. This will require of course some mechanical engineering knowledge but also electrical engineering and software familiarity. Beyond this, there will develop a thriving business in robot deployment, rental, and customization for specific purposes.

Many years ago, I worked for a company that developed, manufactured, and sold high-resolution D and E-sized printers. Using vector and raster technology, these units, some priced as high as $60,000, were needed by integrated circuit developers, mapmakers, architects, and others who had to have high resolution printouts. But our company was knocked out of the saddle when inkjet disrupted the business, and although inkjet could not compete in terms of high resolution, customers saved enough money to switch anyway.

Many of the people that had marketing and engineering 2-D printing knowledge went to work for Stratasys and other 3-D printing companies that built three-dimensional products by depositing layers of particles. Today, you can "print" a small part needed in a manufacturing subassembly all the way up to an automobile, although high cost remains an obstacle in the business. But as technological breakthroughs will be forthcoming, as they always are, costs will come down and this industry is going to boom.

Earlier in the text I discussed the manufacturing project I worked on with a boutique, high-tech operations consulting company called Pittiglio-Rabin-Todd-McGrath (now PwC). Not long after that project, I left my vice president position at Seagate and joined the consulting firm. I enjoyed the tough problems at our client tech companies and found consulting to be a richly rewarding endeavor. You can create flexible schedules and pick and choose your projects. Technology is changing rapidly, and every business today must have its own online presence. Consultants are going to be in high demand as advisors and guides to people in healthcare, finance, law, human resources, marketing, and many other areas. Pick a passion, become a subject matter expert and either start your own firm or join up with others to consult in your chosen field or even some of the fields mentioned earlier.

Gen Z and Millennials

Much has been written as characterizing younger people can take the form of both negative and positive attributes claimed to valid generalizations. We cover a few that hopefully will provide enough input to get a sense of the kinds of jobs and businesses that these folks are hoping to grow into. The coming generation soon to enter the workplace is Gen Z. The U.S. Census Bureau reports that Gen Z (post-Millennial generation) makes up 25 percent of our population. Sixty-two percent of Gen Z are expecting challenges with working successfully alongside Baby Boomers and

Figure 8.1 Social Media—Organic—Service Business

Gen X, though only 5 percent anticipate challenges working alongside Millennials.[1]

The parents of Gen Z suffered through the Great Recession and saw their net worth almost cut in half. So, the children have a stoic sense of realism when it comes to making, saving, and investing money. This book recommends that as you are preparing to go to work or to start a new business, that your horizon primarily comprehends Millennials and Gen Z. Though it seems that much continues to be written about the bulge we call Baby Boomers, the last of them (born in 1964) are soon going to be turning 60.

Three out of four Gen Z folks agree with the advice, "If you want it done right, you better do it yourself." That alone speaks volumes. While Millennials tend to be more tribal and collaborative, Gen Z are more independent and want their own space and opportunities to chase success. When we talk about the Internet, search, messaging, and digital devices all, Gen Z was born into these, they know nothing about the predecessor means of performing these activities and have no reason to care.

With the advent of social media, came the outpouring of the souls of the Millennial. From selfies to personal experiences, they poured out into the public domain more about themselves than their family and closest friends ever knew. Contrast that to the Gen Z man or woman, who eschew "opening up" and jealously guard their private lives. The primary reason Gen Z choose Snapchat is so their information that goes out expires in due course rather than living on in perpetuity and infamy, as the case may be. Gen Z also know that today's HR software can cull, sift, and screen all applicants' online public posts and comments. As a LinkedIn user myself, after reading some alarming and inflammatory posts, that fact should give people pause when it comes to politics, religion, and ideological opinions in general.

In the pandemic, we witnessed great colleges and universities going online, students remotely used Zoom for their classes. At roughly $50,000 tuition, and students graduating with the albatross of a quarter million in debt around their necks, Gen Z is questioning that model and no longer believes it is required for success. Remember, anything that can be taught at university is today available online through YouTube, Google Scholar, e-reader books and a variety of resources that you pick and choose specifically for your chosen field. Finally, in the midst of America turning inward and becoming increasingly isolationist, Gen Z views the world through the lens of the Internet, their purview is a global perspective.

Socialism

Today, we have a yawning wealth gap to contend with. The top 10 percent of income earners are gobbling up half of the income stream in the United States. And in the past few years, this gap has grown even more as the monetary stimulus from the Federal Reserve has benefited Wall Street and hardly helped Main Street. Beginning with the 1980's income growth among the majority of Americans has been almost nonexistent, while the majority of income growth has accrued among the top 10 percent, especially the top 1 percent, creating a dichotomy of many billionaires while over half of Americans have less than $1,000 to their name.

Historically, when a society stratifies wealth and income to such extremes, with a CEO making hundreds of times more than the workers in the company, societal discontent and discord take shape. One outcome is the newfound interest in socialism. Socialism promises a more fair and just distribution of the productive output of a nation. Today, it is called by other less inflammatory terms such as democratic socialism, progressivism, or collectivism, many proponents, young and old are supporting some form of it. Even in the government, Bernie Sanders and Alexandria

Income Distribution (Pre-tax)

How U.S. earners' hsares of the total household income pie have changed

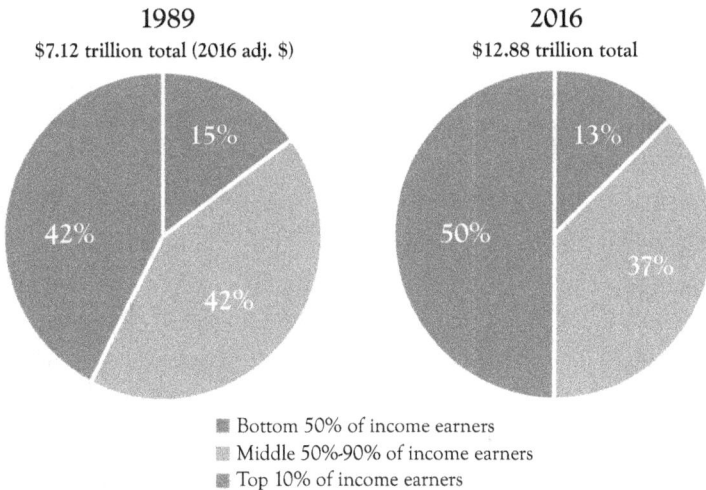

1989	2016
$7.12 trillion total (2016 adj. $)	$12.88 trillion total

Bottom 50% of income earners
Middle 50%-90% of income earners
Top 10% of income earners

■ FEDERAL RESERVE BANK OF ST. LOUIS

Figure 8.2 Income distribution

Ocasio-Cortez, are clearly in that camp and getting traction. That history does not give high marks to nations that tried socialism in the past, the huge wealth gap is reinvigorating the ideology.

Modern-Monetary Theory (MMT) and Universal Basic Income (UBI) are two instances of government transfers of wealth from the rich to the poor. The pandemic exacerbated those on the verge of becoming completely impoverished, and a combination of stimulus, extended unemployment benefits, and additional unemployment amounted to trillions transferred from increased government debt into the hands and pockets of the needy. Expect this trend to continue as we move from a Republican Administration to a Democrat as the new Commander-in-Chief for 2021.

As both monetary and fiscal stimulus in the face of the pandemic-induced recession led to waves of trillions in government assistance, the government effectively took control over much of the financial sector, determining asset values and income streams. The Fed even began purchasing high-yield debt securities, otherwise known as junk bonds, effectively creating zombie companies. The zombies are technically insolvent but are today enabled to continuously roll over their debt in order to avoid shutting down completely. This new socialism came on the watch of a Republican president, so the trend appears to have nonpartisan support.

Climate Change

Companies are under pressure when it comes to climate change. While they may have had a bit of a 4-year hiatus under President Trump, a vocal climate-change denier, all that is about to change under President Biden, who sees climate change as the world's number one joint challenge. The *Extinction Rebellion* last year, in 2019, six million people from 180 countries jointly participated in street protests timed to the September United Nation Climate Summit.[2] School walkouts had been occurring throughout the year.

The fears associated with climate change have extended to financial stability. The Task Force on Climate-related Financial Disclosures (TCFD) formed in 2015, and also the Network for Greening the Financial System (NGFS) came two years later. Both deal with the need for more awareness, transparency, and risk management and transparency in terms of the ramifications of climate change.

When it comes to climate change, there is growing awareness among companies that they are facing serious business risks. From impacts arising from water shortages and the effects of extreme weather to changes in regulations and technologies. For example, what happens if (when?) companies begin to get fined or assessed according to their contributions to greenhouse gases (GHG)? We are seeing an increase in the number of legal cases that have been brought against fossil fuel companies and utilities.

Environmental emissions programs such as the Zero Emissions Vehicle (ZEV) program in California, issue credits to automakers that sell electric vehicles. Besides California, there are currently 13 other U.S. states with similar programs. If an automaker lacks sufficient credits at year-end, it faces fines from state regulators.

Tesla produces only EVs, the company generates far more credits beyond the minimum regulatory requirements, then it can sell excess credits to other automakers so that they avoid penalties. Fiat Chrysler reportedly committed to buying $1.3 billion in credits from Tesla in order to comply with the new European environmental regulations effective 2021.

Climate change also offers several business opportunities. Companies can improve resource productivity (increasing energy efficiency), which in turn may reduce costs. Innovation too, in the form of new products less carbon-rich, and companies can address their supply chains, reducing the current reliance on fossil fuels by moving further toward renewable energy alternatives.

Green, Eco-Friendly, and Organic

From climate change, we naturally segue into the emphasis today on going *green*. Large companies have their corporate sustainability objectives, but smaller firms? Not so much. Yet smaller means easier in terms of adoption, so we cover some of the trends in this section. Research has shown that small business green initiatives provide a distinct competitive edge.[3] Green products and services are more profitable than conventional ones, as customers are willing to spend more. Today, most people expect that the business they engage with is doing everything they can to be eco-friendly. Eco-friendly companies generate customer goodwill while the further away from eco-friendly a company is the worse they will be seen in terms of customer ill-will.

Reputation is probably the most valuable asset any business has. Small businesses will continue to be in business only if word-of-mouth is favorable since experiences on social media and review sites are widely shared among consumers. When my daughter goes to the supermarket with me, she will always grab the product that is *all-natural*. It may be the dog food that costs more, or it may be cleaning products that also cost more. But with her, I have become acutely aware that my grocery store has dedicated shelf space to consumers who are environmentally sensitive. The fact is that some people will boycott any business that is deceptive about their green products.

Creativity and innovation can lead to entirely new green products in addition to moving your current business, products and service in that general direction. A niche market can be bootstrapped, offering products that are brand new and eco-friendly. Frugalpac, a UK company that makes packaging for liquids, developed a recycled-paper coffee cup, this along with their innovative paper wine bottle, made entirely from 94 percent recycled paper, led to new opportunities and partnerships, as well as government grants. Millennials and Gen Z, especially, are keen to get on with these types of initiatives and ways of doing business.

Corporate Social Responsibility

Corporate social responsibility (CSR) is the business model that enables a company to be socially accountable to stakeholders and to the general public. Corporate citizenship has been added to the goals and objectives of companies beyond growth and profitability, as companies are now being measured by their impact on society, in terms of the economic, social, and environmental aspects. Engaging in CSR means the company is seeking positive effects on society and the environment rather than contributing negatively to them.

Corporate social responsibility as a concept can take several forms depending on the type of company and the industry within which they operate. Examples include philanthropy, and volunteer efforts, community outreach, and other activities and investments that benefit the community, and in turn boost the company's brand.

When CSR first got started, most companies simply added a CSR page to their corporate website. They made generalized altruistic claims about business practices and moral and ethical obligations much as you might find on any conference room wall stated on a plaque. But as CSR activities gained traction and garnered increasing credibility, the stakeholders, including investors, employees, customer, and suppliers, all began to demand not only CSR but genuine demonstration in the form of concrete steps taken to prove the company takes CSR seriously. Some companies showed the rest how to do CSR. Starbucks, for example, is known as a leader when it comes to creating corporate social responsibility programs in many aspects of its business. With only a passing nod to CSR, that will contribute to morale issues among employees today, particularly those younger people who take this very seriously and want to see actions that go along with the words.

Corporate Corruption

From CSR, we have to broach its antithesis: *corporate corruption*. Earlier in the book we gave several examples of egregious corruption, so much so in some companies that it became their culture, and a culture is very difficult to change. America is experiencing a downward trajectory in terms of losing the value of virtuous and ethical business practices, indeed news articles of outrageously fraudulent activities seem to be almost a daily diet, much to our shame. The problem with a slow, inexorable slide into expanding and further corruption is that a nation can become so far gone that it is weakened, and history teaches that it will finally collapse or be otherwise destroyed. This is an alarming trend, and unless we can turn it around, America will sink from its superpower perch as other nations pass us by and take our place on the global stage.

Enron is a story of frauds and defalcations that many people remember. From 1996 to 2001, Enron vastly overstated their profitability.

Once the ruse was uncovered, the company filed for bankruptcy and several of the officers went to prison. But since that time, we have witnessed similar misdeeds from Citibank, ESPN, Tyco, WorldCom, the New York Yankees, Exxon Mobil, and ChevronTexaco. In some cases, businesses were dealing with entities that were prohibited. Corporate fraud seems to rise and later fall with new legislation such as the 2002 Corporate Reform bill. But that is only a reset and we see again and again business behaving badly, driven by greed and the drive for financial success.

An entire book could be dedicated to the continuous parade of crime in corporate cultures. We could go all the way back to the Rockefellers, the Vanderbilt's, and the JP Morgan's when the term *robber barons* became en vogue. Corporate corruption is expensive, in terms of higher costs of regulation, scrutiny, and oversight. Also, the company uses profits on their legal defense, their brand is hurt, a great many areas are negatively impacted financially. Probably the most important step to take is to make prison time more common. For most companies, corruption is a cost of doing business. If they get away with their shenanigans, they prosper. If they get caught, which likely is not too often, they pay an entirely affordable fine and turn the expense into a D&O insurance claim for reimbursement.

CHAPTER 9

Saving and Investing

Saving

As I write this book, former Vice President Joe Biden has won the 2020 election and is preparing to take office in January 2021. A quote from him would be a good way to kick off the subject of this chapter: "Don't tell me what you value, show me your budget, and I'll tell you what you value." We can learn a great deal about a person if we learn how they spend what they earn. We can learn even more if we also see people spending more, sometimes far more than they earn. The next and last chapter will deal with debt. Debt has become a four-letter word anchoring our economy and hindering future growth.

When I was young, I never had much. My dad came off a farm and started a little construction business in rural Wisconsin. It seemed like he was always working, but a family of 8 children were not seeing the fruits of Dad's labor. I made myself a promise—that I would pursue a career that made enough money that I would never again be in poverty and that my children would have enough inheritance to start whatever passion and career they wanted to pursue.

During the Great Depression, many people watched in horror as their farms were being repossessed by banks through foreclosure. The current decade we are in has much in common with that period in history. The result of the suffering and poverty and bankruptcies of the Great Depression led to a long-lasting behavioral change in the people. Those emerging from the Depression and World War II were frugal. They eschewed brands, luxuries and focused their finances on necessities, value and saving. They worked hard, saved a lot, bought homes, had large families, and in general, put significant value on the virtues of honesty, integrity, character, humility, moderation, working for a living, saving and caring for family, and community.

Fast forward to the 2020s. Things have really changed, and not for the better. The values of people today have shifted dramatically. A transient workforce has resulted in oftentimes cutting the long-term ties to families and old friends. My little town of Waukesha, Wisconsin was just fine for most of my friends who remained there, but I moved to Austin, Texas and later to California because that is where the tech jobs and good salaries were. At this writing, I am planning my return to Wisconsin, although to those I grew up with I am mostly a stranger.

Beginning around the 1980s, the economic and financial behavior and choices began to change. Although slowly at first, I became aware that people seemed to be living well beyond their means. Administrative assistants were driving Mercedes and BMW's, financed with long-term leases. Folks were spending hundreds of dollars on a pair of brand-name jeans. What the great philosopher Thorstein Veblen referred to as *conspicuous consumption* had taken hold of the society in a dramatic and big way. Credit card balances were growing and so was the interest being charged. But the high lifestyle became the status quo and peer pressure pushed the buying trends into high gear. The Christmas shopping season that once began a few weeks before Christmas was pushed back to the day after Thanksgiving, otherwise known as Black Friday.

The conspicuous consumption satisfied at the malls has turned online in the pandemic. Today Amazon, Costco, Walmart and Target's online businesses are booming. Studies done after government money went out to people—many of whom were unemployed in the pandemic—showed that purchases of electronics and other discretionary purchases dominated commerce, rather than purchasing necessities and adding to savings accounts.

One in four Americans, 25 percent of the population have not saved enough to cover even two months of expenses, according to research. While the vast majority polled recognize the importance of saving, one in four don't even have a savings account.[1] The importance of saving cannot be overemphasized. In the past, companies provided pensions for retirement. Today the 401(k) has replaced the pension. Social security is designed only to cover about 40 percent of one's expenses through retirement. A good rule of thumb as a savings goal for retirement is $2 million in the bank and your home mortgage completely paid off. Yet, the vast majority of Americans will never get there.

Worse, savings accounts that decades ago, and for quite a long time, paid 5 percent interest on the standard passbook saving account, today pay maybe a tenth of one percent, not even enough to cover inflation. At 5 percent interest rate, a savings amount will double in under 15 years, but at almost zero interest rate, only what you put in the account is what you will have to spend later in life. While that understandably sounds discouraging, unless you plan to learn how to enjoy dog food, you had better get on with it while you are still gainfully employed and can save.

Save at least 10 percent of your gross income and strive to save more. Save every cash gift, bonus and unexpected windfall, all of it. Select at least 10 percent withholding for your 401(k), but make it higher if it means the company match will also be higher. You want all of what the company match can provide based upon your own company benefits. Don't say you cannot afford it. You can certainly afford it, even if that means you have to figure out how to do without other things, how to find cheap transportation and even if you must forget about ever owning a home. It is all about your own determination and willingness to plan for your future, and excuses will only result in a miserable twilight of your life.

Investing

I taught finance at a local university for 4 years. I was appalled at the lack of even basic fundamental financial knowledge. It was obvious that K-12 public education completely omitted this crucial part of teaching. Not long ago, I created a high school finance class syllabus, posted to my online LinkedIn account and mailed it to local high schools. My letter of introduction included the offer to teach high school students finance for free. No charge. I would be an unpaid high school teacher. None even bothered to respond to me, so you can see how oblivious our public school system is to the importance of teaching finance. That is tragic and explains why people are struggling with their own household budgets today.

MBA programs will teach concepts such as how capital flows to the best and most efficient uses, stocks have averaged good returns over the long run and bonds—while having lower long-term returns than stocks—are safer, particularly the U.S. Treasury bonds. Unfortunately, today none of that matters, as none of it applies any longer. The model of capitalism you may have studied with companion books written by Adam Smith or Ayn Rand are no longer useful today, as the world of investing has become radically different, a result of monetary and fiscal intrusions on a massive scale.

A couple of extreme examples should suffice to make my point in terms of how one can no longer rely upon the old rules of investing. This is a frustrating period that we are in, a time of economic and financial uncertainty the likes of which we have not seen nor experienced since the Great Depression of the 1930s. Worse, it appears the government largesse is an assault on the currency, and that in due course will impact even the cash you have squirreled away for a rainy day. Let's begin with the stock market today:

Stocks

Amazon. AMZN. In the past year, Amazon has traded between $1,626 and $3,552 and is up 70 percent year-to-date. Amazon is a great company and is crushing the competition. With $350 billion in annual revenue and a market capitalization of well over $1.5 trillion, people are naturally drawn to invest in the stock. But history tells us that the market, over a long period of time, generally trades at 15 to 16 times earnings. Amazon is trading at 91 times their earnings, and growing revenue at a rate of 37 percent. But at this size, if Amazon's growth rate averaged only 20 percent per year, and their market cap grew at that rate, in 20 years, Amazon would have a market cap of almost $50 trillion, or two and a half times the entire U.S. GDP. Conclusion: Great company, highly successful, but the stock price is twice or more what is a reasonable valuation.

Robinhood

A year ago, some of the retail stock trading platforms changed their policies to zero-commission. This meant the layperson could trade night and day without ever paying a commission fee. In due course, most of the retail platforms such as e-Trade and Charles Schwab followed the pioneer Robinhood and eliminated their commission fee structure as well. Then came the pandemic.

The pandemic hit gamblers of all stripes hard. Casinos and horse race-tracks were closed. Betting on professional sports disappeared. So, the friendly and intuitive smartphone app called Robinhood became a gambling avocation for many. Robinhood is a free-trading app for investors who want to trade stocks, stock options, cryptocurrency, and exchange-traded funds without paying commissions or fees of any kind. The service is innovative, friendly, and intuitive, cutting out most of the costs typically associated with investing.

Dave Portnoy of Barstool Sports began gambling with Robinhood. Overtime, he amassed a Twitter following of 1.8 million. He would select the stocks to purchase, then tout those stocks to his Twitter followers who dutifully bought these stocks in large quantities. Over time the retail stock crowd began to buy on margin, essentially borrowing money to buy these select favorite stocks. They then moved into buying call options, a risky investment that allows a person to buy a certain quantity of a stock at a strike price, though the option carries an expiration date. Margin buying and option trading are a leveraged means of making more money, but they are also far riskier than simply buying the underlying stock. Some strange and perverse market machinations resulted from the retail gamblers, two of which we discuss next:

Tesla. TSLA. In the past year, Tesla has traded between $65 and $302 and has a market cap that is higher than any other auto company in the world. But Tesla receives hundreds of millions from government for their clean energy (EV) vehicles. Those regulatory credits have amounted to over $1 billion and are booked as revenue that drops at 100 percent to the bottom-line earnings when they sell their credits to other manufacturers who aren't keeping up with government-edicted clean energy vehicle initiatives. If you remove the credits, they sell to other car manufacturers. Tesla has never made a profit. Not in the 17 years they have been in business. And the Tesla PE (price-earnings) ratio? A whopping 780 times earnings. While this company certainly has value, their market cap of almost $400 billion is ten times larger than can be financially justified.

Carvana. CVNA. Carvana sell used cars online, a hit during the pandemic, resulting in a range in stock price from a low of $22 to a high of $242 in the past year. Carvana has never made a profit, only losses. While their unit sales surged as people flocked to buy used cars online in the midst of the pandemic, and even more so as fears of public transportation drove them to car ownership, the company does not have a business model that can generate profitability, not at any high volume.

The point is that stocks in general are today in what we refer to as a *bubble*. The prices are simply too high relative to the earnings, meaning a market correction will be appearing in due course and a lot of people will see wealth significantly reduced when that happens. Speculators are as prevalent and giddy today as they were just prior to the dot-com market crater. There is an apparent expectation that with the advent of a vaccine, the economy will snap back to pre-pandemic status. That won't happen and we will talk about just why in the next and last chapter.

Finally, there are many twists, turns, combinations, and related ways to bet on stock values. You can buy options to purchase a stock at a certain price, but these have an expiration date. You can sell stock while delaying the purchase side of the transactions, expecting to be able to make your purchase at a lower price. But these transactions carry additional risk. Options expire, shorting a stock may result in you having to finally make the stock purchase at an unanticipated much higher price. I don't recommend these derivative, exotic, and risky transactions except for a select few of highly experienced traders.

Caveat Emptor. Let the Buyer Beware.

Bonds

Bonds are generally held up as safer than stocks. Bonds are debt, debt of the nation in the form of U.S. Treasuries, and debt of a company that uses the proceeds as a part of their capital structure in the case of corporate bonds. The interest rate on U.S. Treasuries was considered a riskless rate as the government is not likely to default on paying bonds at the date they mature. That rate has generally been around 4 percent for 10-year Treasury's. For corporate bonds, the interest they must pay to get all the bonds issued and sold is a riskless rate plus a risk premium. Risk is rated by agencies, from stellar and sound (AAA) all the way down to the high-yield speculative bonds also called *junk bonds*.

Today, a lot of bonds that have been issued are trading at prices that have market rates close to zero, even a negative market rate. Why would someone buy a bond with an implied negative rate of interest? Isn't that like paying the creditor who is using and risking your money? Not if you expect the rate to go further negative, increasing the value of the bond you just bought, for bond prices move inversely with their rates. Since the 1980s, the United States has embarked on a steady climb up a mountain of debt, and from an economic standpoint, a debt-soaked economy is going to suppress and reduce interest rates. These rates have been steadily declining for the past 40 years.

The effect of formerly high-yielding, high-risk bonds having interest rates near zero is to imply there is zero risk to those holding these bonds as an investment. This assurance has come about as the Federal Reserve has been stepping in to buy these bonds in an effort to keep their ZIRP (zero interest rate policy) intact in order to stimulate the economy. But without that monetary intrusion, the value of these bonds would collapse, and the market interest rates would rocket higher to capture risk premiums. The investor again must beware, for the Federal Reserve to keep this scenario going in perpetuity, it must keep buying the same or increasing levels of these bonds. Once again, we conclude that bond prices are in a *bubble*. The prices are too high, and the risk is too great.

Caveat Emptor. Let the Buyer Beware.

Gold (Precious Metals)

Gold has been a currency and store of value for thousands of years. Gold coins first appeared around 800 B.C.; the first pure gold coins were minted during the time of King Croesus of Lydia 300 years later. People have owned gold for various reasons. It is the gold we retreat to when other forms of currency break down, a value that is essentially considered insurance through the tough times.

Although, like silver, gold is a commodity with utility and industrial uses, it is viewed as a special and valuable commodity. During inflationary times, as a currency loses its purchasing power, gold acts as a hedge against inflation as well as a portfolio diversifier. Other reasons to explain the flight to gold are during periods of geopolitical and macroeconomic uncertainty. When currency appears to have significant risks, inflation or otherwise, gold investors are comfortable owning the metal and bequeathing their gold to heirs and future generations without worrying about the currency. Gold won't corrode and can be transformed into coins, ingots, bars, jewelry, or just about any shape imaginable.

The supply of gold has come from sales of gold bullion mostly originating in the vaults of global central banks. Production of new gold from mines has been on the decline for the past couple decades. BullionVault.com annual gold-mining output decreased from 2,573 tons in the year 2000 to about 2,444 tons seven years later. It can take from 5 to 10 years to bootstrap a new mine into production, so the supply constraint will also result in the value of gold increasing. In these times of huge government deficits and geo-political tensions, gold, along with silver and miners' stocks, are a good long-term safe harbor investment.

Bitcoin

Contrast to gold, Bitcoin has been around only 10 years. The digital currency is underpinned by a groundbreaking new technology called Blockchain. Blockchain is a means of protecting transactions and data through the decentralization of records across member computers. This compares to the vulnerability of a central database that can be hacked. Blockchain is complex in terms of the math but suffice to say the technology is presenting itself as almost ubiquitous and research is underway to use Blockchain to authenticate identification, develop smart contracts, and many other possibilities.

Having studied the price movements of Bitcoin for a decade, I have found no underlying consistent exogenous variable to account for its price movements. It appears to be as random as playing craps in a casino. But it can go up very high, so the lure of making a lot of money keeps people engaged, and consequently, keeps the demand high enough that the transaction volume continues to be high. Comparisons to gold are being made today as government is giving away trillions in stimulus and financial assistance, worrying people about the stability of the U.S. dollar. Bitcoin in 2020 has gone up considerably in price as a result of this concern and the desire to seek out safe harbor if the currency should fail.

Today, countries such as China are developing their own cryptocurrencies. Most commerce is electronic today anyway, but the cryptocurrency will finally take the paper and coins and obsolete these in the future. The path starts with a government-sanctioned plan, followed by the empowerment of their corresponding monetary authority for regulating, tracking, auditing, and protecting transactions, and then a date future gets set when the nation's currency will no longer be legal tender.

From this, we can conclude that Bitcoin, Ethereum, or any of the dozens of cryptocurrencies today, while instructive and informative to the world when it comes to rolling out their own cryptocurrencies, none of these will ever replace any nation's fiat currency. That process begins with government, so we can expect today's cryptocurrencies will be a fun gambling casino for a long while but will never fill the shoes as a long-term asset or generally accepted currency.

Caveat Emptor. Let the Buyer Beware.

Commodities, Collectibles and Other Asset Investments

When investors fear stocks and bonds are overpriced, as they clearly are today, and at the same time believe the currency is at risk, creating an aversion to holding cash, they turn to collectibles. These are generally assets whose values have remained or gone up over a long period of time, and the investor is well-versed—knows the asset category quite well. The range in almost infinite, as they include fine wine, paintings, sculptures, musical instruments, baseball trading cards, antiques, classic cars, rare coins, and other hard-to-find and limited supply assets whose values have withstood the test of time.

Conclusion

The year 2020 is unique and filled with a lot of emotion-driven investing decisions tied to expectations regarding the final outcome of the pandemic. Stocks and bonds are very risky today and until they come back to historical valuation metrics, stay away. Likewise, Bitcoin is gambling, although its proponents will argue as fervently as any cult that the cryptocurrency will ultimately replace all the world's fiat currencies.

That leaves only cash and gold, and even cash is risky as the currency is under assault as the waves of trillions in free money continues from 2020 into 2021. Timing is crucial and stocks and bonds will return as attractive investments following market correction. Until then, consider some amount of cash, gold, and collectibles and wait until post-pandemic and a return to growth. Unfortunately, the return to growth is going to be quite a long way off, for the reasons we provide in the last chapter on DEBT.

CHAPTER 10

Post-pandemic, Debt, and De-Leveraging

Earlier we spoke of the new savings behavioral patterns our previous generation adopted as a result of losing homes and farms to foreclosure during the Great Depression almost a century ago. Savings and frugality replaced speculation and debt, and for almost a half century, America made a virtue out of the value of avoiding spending money on frivolous things, saving as much as possible and steering clear of speculative ventures and investments. A conservative economic ideology ruled and reigned up until the 1980s.

Beginning in the 80s, however, the trend began to move away from frugality and a simple life toward conspicuous consumption. But since earnings were insufficient to fund a life of expensive brands, discretionary purchases, expensive entertainment, and travel options, and keeping up with others by figuring out how to drive an expensive car, leases, credit cards, loans, and debt in general became the means to a standard of living that increasingly over the subsequent years exceeded our earnings.

If today you would claim that "debt is good," a great many others would agree with you, as the debt is almost free, and the use of that money appears to be unavoidable. In fact, the opposite is true. Debt is nothing more than borrowing from future earnings. Another way to say that is living beyond one's means today means living below one's earnings in the future. But the insidious nature of debt is that the new higher total spending and consumption becomes the expectation, necessitating ever-increasing loads of debt to keep the economic status quo. Today, we have record levels of debt, so much so in fact that mathematically it is impossible to ever repay it all in total. Let's look at the components of the pervasive debt that has impacted ever level and sector in—not just America—but throughout the entire world.

National Debt

In times of war, we understandably resorted to debt to finance the war effort. In the case of the UK, they had tremendous postwar debt, in part because they were heavily bombed. But it was this excessive debt that led to the collapse of the British Pound Sterling, much as happened prior to that with the Dutch Guilder. Over-reach and overindebtedness were the underlying causes.

Beginning with the GFC, the Federal Reserve embarked on a plan referred to as Quantitative Easing (QE). The intention was to reduce the cost of borrowing money, the interest rate, to stimulate economic growth. In addition, massive amounts of liquidity were provided to member banks so lending would increase and speed the economic recover.

This backfired, however, although that only became apparent when the Federal Reserve (Fed) sought to reduce the amount of U.S. Treasuries and Mortgage-Backed Securities they were purchasing to push down interest rates. Known as the "taper tantrum," credit markets reacted swiftly by ratcheting up interest rates, causing the Fed to halt the effort to reduce their investments on their balance sheet.

Since that time, and most especially lately with the pandemic-caused recession, the Fed has added trillions to their balance sheet, even

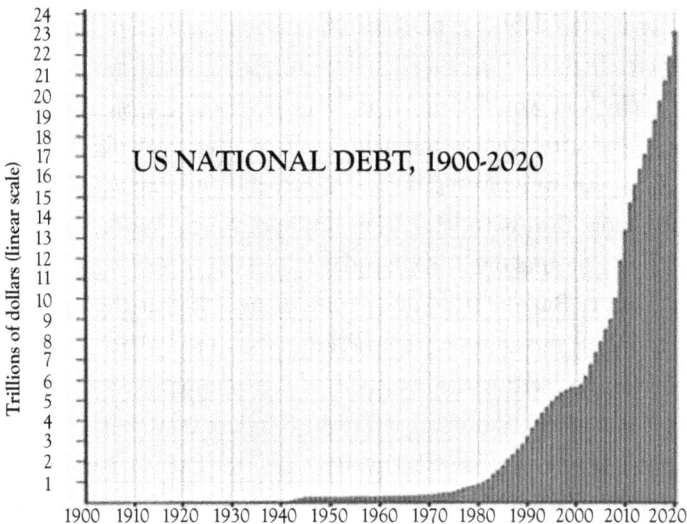

Figure 10.1 National Debt

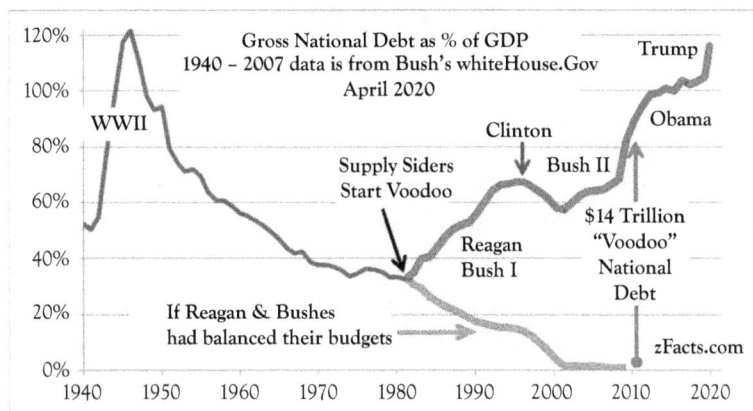

Figure 10.2 *Debt percentage of GDP*

purchasing high-yield speculative bond funds in an effort to keep their zero-interest rate policy (ZIRP) from losing control over what they hoped would lead to an economic recovery post-pandemic.

What the Fed failed to take into consideration, apparently, was that excessive, unproductive debt will reduce GDP growth, lower interest rates, and create a disinflationary economy.[1] Going back to the 1980s, we see a decade of 4 percent GDP growth, followed by a decade of 3 percent GDP growth, last decade clocked in at 2 percent GDP growth, and the 2020s will likely only register 0 to 1 percent GDP growth. And the 40-year period experienced a steady decline in interest rates and its corresponding increase in the value of bonds, taking bonds, like stocks, into entirely risky and unjustifiable valuations today. The frightening prospect is twofold. First, in the event of war, the national debt would skyrocket and eventually the currency would collapse. Secondly, most economists believe that each new incremental dollar of debt is no longer producing growth. In other words, more debt is not helping, but only hindering and hurting. Once a nation's debt exceeds about 90 percent of GDP, it loses is productive punch. Today, American's national debt is approaching 125 percent of GDP.

This is not purely an American policy. Central banks around the world have been supplying massive amounts of stimulus and liquidity in the attempts to kick their economies into a higher gear. It hasn't worked. Today, over 90 percent of the nations of the world are in recession and the ointment and balm they continue to apply comes from more debt, which in turn only exacerbates a problem of slow growth, decreasing interest rates and disinflation. Until and unless some amount of pain associated with intentional deleveraging, creating a period of tough austerity, is finally resorted to, government policy is only kicking the debt can down the road and making the ultimate deleveraging pain that much worse when deleveraging is finally forced upon the nations. For we have reached the point where incremental additions to debt are no longer having an intended stimulative effect on any economy.

Debt is increasing rapidly on every continent as borrowing this past decade has risen to previously unheard-of levels. The International Monetary Fund (IMF) said that 40 percent of the debt is in eight leading countries—the United States, China, Japan, Britain, Germany, Italy, France, and Spain. The math indicates the debt load has become virtually impossible to service. Essentially, said another way, the world has become insolvent. The World Bank agrees. It said that the combination of emerging-market and developing economies (EMDE's) had pushed borrowing to a record $55 trillion in 2018.

The greatest threat that is of a more immediate concern is the stability of currency. As the dominant world reserve currency, the United States is in the catbird seat apparently not worried about debasing their currency. This may be true for a while because almost all other nations are equally economically distressed so there is no obvious world reserve currency alternative waiting in the wings. Over time, this may change as China has been growing faster than the United States and seeks to displace the U.S. Dollar by making their own currency more internationally accepted and more transparent.

Corporate Debt

Likewise, with the lure of lower interest rates, companies have gone on a borrowing binge that continues to the present day. In the past, companies returned capital to shareholders by paying dividends. These dividends were already subject to corporate income tax, and once distributed, they became subject to the income taxes of the recipient shareholders. Companies argued they could increase shareholder wealth more

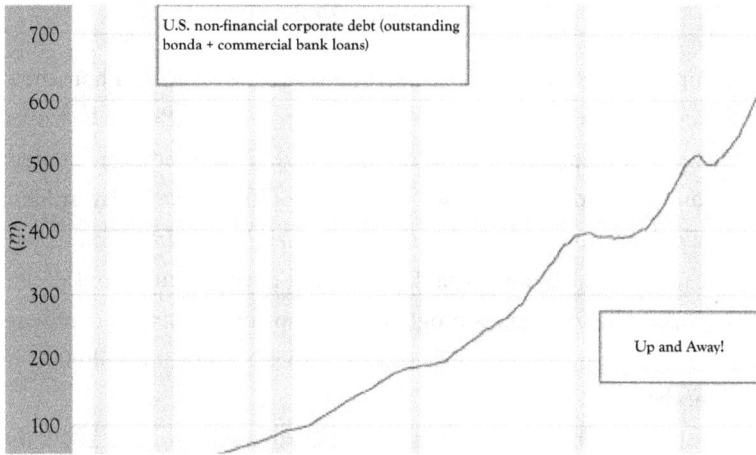

Figure 10.3 Corporate Debt

efficiently by borrowing money on the cheap, buying back their own stock, and that this activity would in turn increase the market value of the company's stock as fewer shares were outstanding and earnings per share went up proportionately.

A key reason interest rates are so low is because of the expectation from investors that the Fed would backstop any liquidity, solvency, or other financial problems threatening the company. By buying up speculative bond funds, the Fed has essentially given *zombie* companies a reason to continue in business. A zombie is technically insolvent but continues to stay in business by perpetually rolling over their debt. This creates the unintended consequence of capital market inefficiency, as capital today no longer flows to the best and highest returning companies and projects. This is one more reason why the U.S. economic growth will be moribund throughout this decade, until the debt issue can be dealt with.

It will take all of this decade to unhook from the massive debt anchor. A beautiful deleveraging is the balance across the three ways to deleverage from the debt. There is an austerity component, which the Fed fervently resists, not willing to inflict economic pain. Then there is debt restructuring activity, such as refinancing debt longer term. Finally, we have money printing, a pastime our Fed and Treasury seem enamored with as waves of trillions wash into the hands of troubled companies and financially desperate households.[2]

Consumer Debt

Consumer debt is what you owe as an individual as a part of a household and the debt is termed *consumer credit*. Sources for this debt can be banks, federal government, credit card, car leases and loans, mortgages, student loan sources, payday loans, pawn shops, and online loans. Today, student loans alone are approaching $2 trillion. Realizing the burden and recognizing much can never be repaid, the federal government is considering various possible forgiveness programs. It is not uncommon for students to leave college and begin their careers with $200,000 to $300,000 in student debt.

Consumer debt hit a record of over $4.2 trillion in February 2020, the month before the pandemic and related recession began. But the federal government allowed a hiatus on debt repayments. From rents to car loans and student debt payments, all were allowed to stop so struggling people could get some financial relief. More than that, the government-edicted payment respite would not allow this increasing bow-wave of debt to be counted as "in default" or in any adverse debt calculation. It is apparent that if the debt holiday added in the accumulation of debt from nonpayment most of 2020, the consumer debt mountain would today top $5 trillion.

Debt can be devastating. If you fall behind making payments, perhaps as a result of a long-term illness, divorce, or loss of a job, you can declare bankruptcy and get off the debt hook (except for student loans). But that will hit hard your credit score (FICO). The strange place we find ourselves in the pandemic today, however, is FICO scores are increasing, as debt forbearance programs prohibit reporting defaults as adverse.

A few metrics related to consumer debt[3]:

- Consumer debt totaled $4.1 trillion in Q3'2019
- Average consumer debt is $12,687 per capita in 2020
- Revolving consumer debt totaled $1.1 trillion in late 2019
- Ten percent of adults carry a credit card balance over $5,000
- Student loans were $1.7 trillion in Q3'2019 with an average $82,170
- Auto loans were $1.2 trillion in Q3'2019.

Consumer Bebt 2018-19

Consumer debt rose **4.7%** this past year to almost **$4.2 trillion.**

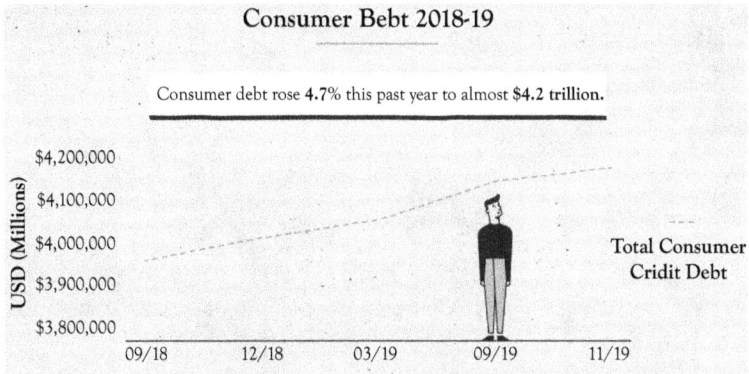

Figure 10.4 Consumer Debt

Final Thoughts on the Economy and Investing

The pandemic has produced a collective view that once the pandemic is past, the economy will return to normal. That is not going to happen. First, as we pointed out earlier, the increasing level of debt that started piling up 40 years ago is the long-term economic disease, the pandemic only accelerated it and obscured what had already been weakening in our economy. Prior to the pandemic, Q4'2019 corporate earnings had already showed considerable weakness.

The pandemic policy of publishing optimistic and hopeful news stories has only served to mislead investors. When a company loses money in a quarter, the news media will oftentimes report that the loss "was not as bad as expected," and the stock price will go up. Likewise, the millions who lost their jobs, expecting to return to these jobs after the vaccine, were classified as "temporarily furloughed," a category not counted in the unemployment numbers. And finally, as alluded to earlier, the bow wave of debt resulting from debt forbearance programs is not considered "in default," although when payments finally resume, these payments will be higher than pre-pandemic in order to catch up and payoff the portion that was forbearance.

The stimulus that began during the Great Recession of a decade ago never stopped. Quite the opposite. The waves of trillions in stimulus from the Treasury and the Fed have continued this year and will continue for the foreseeable future. The stock market has responded favorably to the

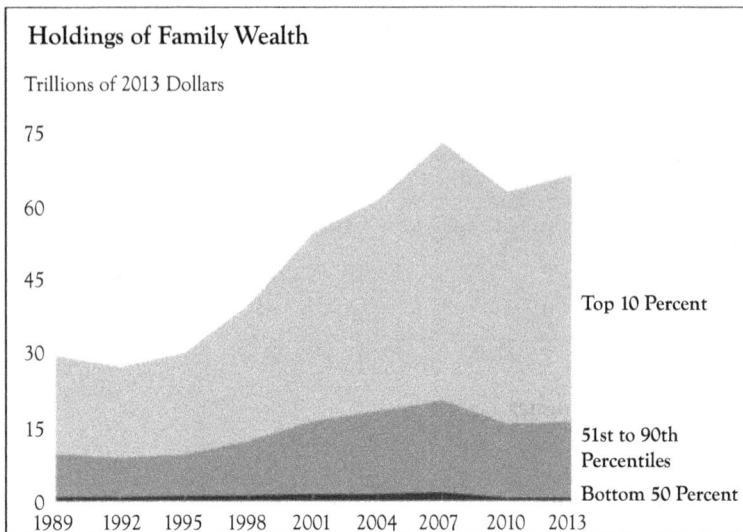

Figure 10.5 Family wealth

injection of liquidity, even though long-term solvency remains a challenge to many companies today.

This stimulus, and the low interest rate policies, along with the lack of fear of inventory risk given the backstopping assistance of government has bid up stock and bond prices well past any possible defensible prices. They are in *bubble territory* and by the time this book is published, we will have experienced or be close to a market correction likely to be a significant meltdown.

In the meantime, the record wealth gap continues to grow. The few have most of the assets and income, and the market distortions have widened that gap significantly further. As of Q3'2019, the bottom 50 percent of individual households had $1.7 trillion, or less than 2 percent of the net worth, versus $75 trillion, or 70 percent of total national net worth for the top 10 percent.[4] Historically, a wealth gap that large has led to civil unrest and even revolutions.

According to a recent research conducted by GoBankingRates.com, nearly half of adult Americans did not have any emergency savings. Three out of four people have less than $5,000 saved, while only 10 percent of respondents had more than $50,000. Over 50 percent of Americans stated they are unprepared financially in the event of a virus like

Distribution of Family Wealth

(2016)

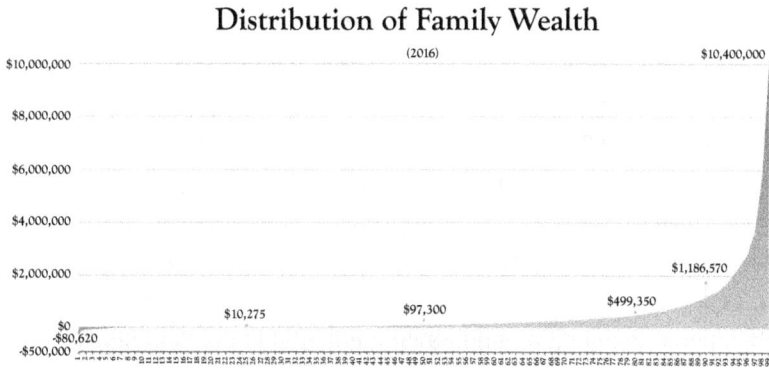

Figure 10.6 *Distribution of family wealth*

Total Wealth of Top 1% and Bottom 50% (1989–2018)

● 1989   ● 2018

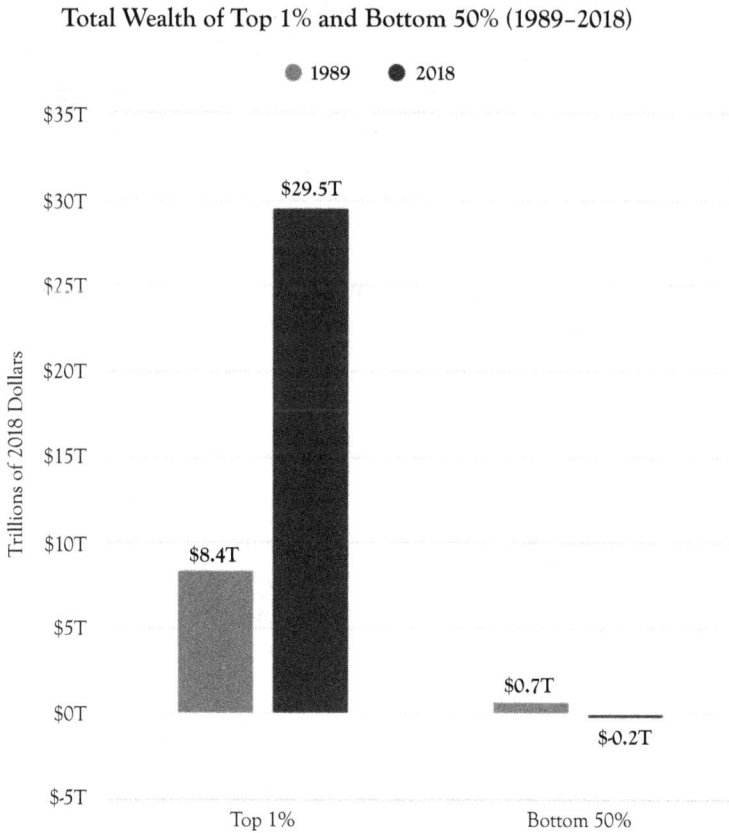

Source: Author's Calculations of Distributive Financial Accounts

Figure 10.7 *Total Wealth by percentage*

COVID-19, if it left them unable to work for several weeks. This survey was conducted at the beginning of March 2020, just as the pandemic was getting underway.

The upcoming year, 2021 will prove challenging. As discussed earlier, savings accounts pay virtually no interest, while stocks and bonds are priced far too high to even consider owning today. The lack of savings and the high unemployment rate will require the continuation of government assistance to individuals and businesses. In due course, the currency will finally take the brunt of all the government giveaways, making even holding of cash a risky proposition as the currency will eventually lose its purchasing power.

The Federal Reserve is trapped with over $7 trillion on its balance sheet. It must continue to purchase U.S. Treasuries and Mortgage-Backed-Securities, or risk increasing interest rates and collapsed asset values. Today, national debt stands at $27 trillion. For each full point increase in interest that means the government must pay an additional $270 billion more. Productive uses of federal spending are being swamped out by the unproductive uses such as entitlements and interest, and this trend will continue. The pressure to cut back on benefits such as Medicaid, Medicare, and Social Security continues to grow as the Baby Boom bulge are almost all applying for these benefits today, and medical technology is keeping them alive far longer.

Inflation

Research has shown that excessive unproductive debt will suppress growth and interest rates and create a disinflationary environment. Today, more than 90 percent of the nations of the world are in this economic trap as central banks have sought to resolve a debt-soaked economic recession by ladling on more debt. As more free money flows to businesses and households, inflation alarms are beginning to be more frequently sounded in the financial press.

But the debt load will prevent inflation. The monetary efforts to stimulate the economy are not working. The tools used are primarily digital dollars deposited into the member banks as the Fed buys more Treasuries and MBS. But if the banks won't lend these reserves, a result of increasing credit requirements in a recession, the effort does not create its intended effect.

Federal Overview Ropriations

federal spending
fy 2018: $4.1 Trillion
(Outlays)

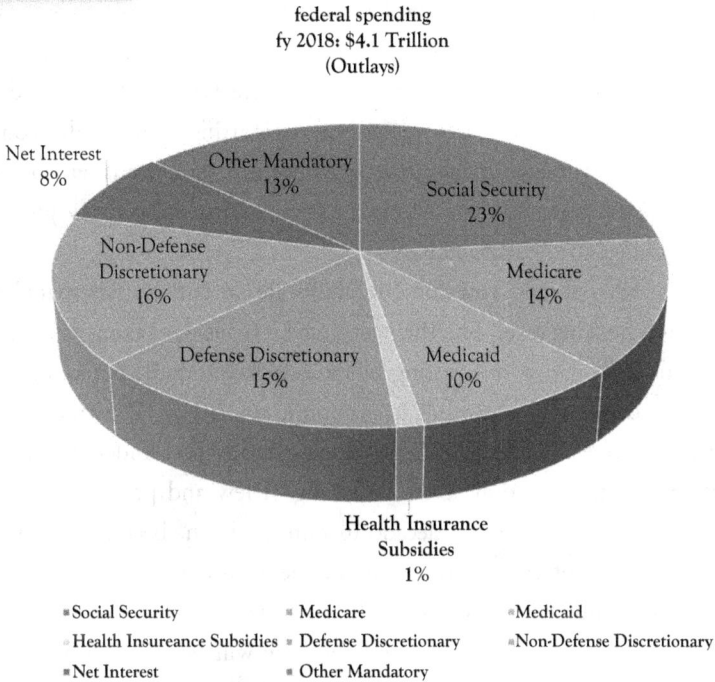

Net Interest 8%

Other Mandatory 13%

Social Security 23%

Non-Defense Discretionary 16%

Medicare 14%

Defense Discretionary 15%

Medicaid 10%

Health Insurance Subsidies 1%

- Social Security
- Medicare
- Medicaid
- Health Insureance Subsidies
- Defense Discretionary
- Non-Defense Discretionary
- Net Interest
- Other Mandatory

Figure 10.8 Federal spending FY 2018

Today, as of this writing, the Fed is considering a scheme that bypasses the banks and goes directly to the bank accounts of individual Americans. This will be a big change, for instead of lending money the Fed will give it away. It may initially be structured as a "loan" but as we saw with the CARES Act, loans were converted to grants upon meeting certain relatively easy requirements.

Following WWI, Germany was required to make onerous payments as war reparations. The Weimar Republic struggled to abide by the repayment agreement but soon found it virtually impossible to service the debt. The German government then began making the payments with fresh, newly printed currency. This led to hyperinflation and almost destroyed the economy. Likewise, if the Fed follows through with their intentions, the United States will experience not just targeted inflation (2%–3%), but hyperinflation. This is a big step and a huge risk facing 2021.

While a lot of this material may seem pessimistic, particularly in light of all the media articles proclaiming the end of the recession and the imminent deployment of the vaccine, it is intended to warn the prudent saver and investor that today we have many mines to avoid in an economic battlefield. Stocks and bonds are priced far too high. The economy is alive but only with the life support systems of the Federal Reserve and the U.S. Treasury. Interest rates are low but this is artificial, and in due course, the market will correct this artificial imbalance. Americans, except for a small percentage, don't have enough saved and social security just may have to be cut to be affordable.

So, what should you do? The 2020s are an entirely new paradigm, looking nothing at all like the past decade. Consider saving as much as you possibly can and investing in the safe haven gold. Emerging from the pandemic will not result in economic prosperity. The mountain of debt will prevent that. Until deleveraging finally gets underway, we will remain in the economic ditch, resulting in few and poor good investment returns. This is the decade to hunker down, become frugal and avoid the temptation to follow the momentum herds who are foolishly crowding into stocks and bonds. This decade, much like the 1930s, is a decade where those who survive financially will be people who see the handwriting on the wall and take the necessary precautions—a great reckoning from the massive mountain of debt is upon us, the bill has come due, we can no longer avoid the deleveraging that has finally been forced upon us.

Notes

Chapter 1

1. (Simon 2019)
2. (Kikaon September 2018)
3. (Julian 2020)

Chapter 2

1. (Nandi 2020)
2. (Maida November 4, 2020)
3. (Cassidy 2020)
4. (Fuller 2020)

Chapter 3

1. (Adams January 10, 2017)
2. (Browne, CNBC. October 5, 2020)

Chapter 4

1. (Glassdoor Team. January 10, 2020)
2. (Portero December 9, 2011)
3. (Gretchen and Emily April 26, 2018)
4. (Wikipedia)

Chapter 5

1. (Allied Market Research May 2018)
2. (Rigby 2020)
3. (Boxall 2020)
4. (Sabin 2020)
5. (DeFi Rate n.d.)
6. (O'Dell 2020)

Chapter 7

1. (Accenture 2020)
2. (Cornell Hospital Quarterly 2005)

Chapter 8

1. (Jenkins July 2017)
2. (Blohmke, Krick and Coppola December 2019)
3. "Small Business Sustainability Report." 2013

Chapter 9

1. (SWNS January 30, 2020)

Chapter 10

1. "Seeking Alpha." September 2020
2. (Dalio May 2012)
3. "Board of Governors of the Federal Reserve System." November 2020
4. (Board of Governors of the Federal Reserve System. N.d.)

References

2013. "Small Business Sustainability Report." *The Big Green Opportunity for Small Business in the U.S.* https://coolcalifornia.arb.ca.gov/sites/coolcalifornia.org/files/Big-Green-Opportunity-Report-FINAL-WEB.pdf (accessed November 14, 2020).

Accenture. 2020. "Who are the Millennial Shoppers? And What do They Really Want?" https://accenture.com/us-en/insight-outlook-who-are-millennial-shoppers-what-do-they-really-want-retail (accessed November 13, 2020).

Adams, S. January 10, 2017. "Forbes." *GoFundMe Buys Rival CrowdRise.* https://forbes.com/sites/susanadams/2017/01/10 (accessed November 15, 2020).

Allied Market Research. May 2018. "Autonomous Vehicle Market Outlook – 2026." https://alliedmarketresearch.com/autonomous-vehicle-market (accessed November 11, 2020).

Blohmke, J., T. Krick, and M. Coppola. December 2019. "Deloitte Insights." *Feeling the heat? Companies are Under Pressure on Climate Change and Need to do More.* https://www2.deloitte.com/us/en/insights/topics/strategy/impact-and-opportunities-of-climate-change-on-business.html (accessed November 14, 2020).

Board of Governors of the Federal Reserve System. N.d. "Distributional National Accounts." https://federalreserve.gov/releases/z1/dataviz/dfa/distribute/table/ (accessed February 20, 2020).

Boxall, A. 2020. "Digital Trends." *MediaTek's Huge 5G Push is Paying Off, Despite 2020's Efforts to Derail Plans.* https://.digitaltrends.com/mobile/mediatek-interview-rick-tsai-2020-summit/ (accessed November 11, 2020).

Browne, R. CNBC. October 5, 2020. *Crowdcube and Seedrs — Which Let You Buy Shares in Privately-held start-ups — are set to merge* https://cnbc.com/2020/10/05/equity-crowdfunding-platforms-crowdcube-and-seedrs-to-merge.html (accessed November 9, 2020).

Cassidy, N. 2020. "Listen Money Matters." *Should I Sell My Stuff On Amazon Handmade?* https://listenmoneymatters.com/amazon-handmade/ (accessed November 8, 2020).

Cornell Hospital Quarterly. 2005. "Why Restaurants Fail." https://journals.sagepub.com/doi/abs/10.1177/0010880405275598 (accessed November 13, 2020).

Dalio, R. May 2012. "Business Insider. RAY DALIO: America Is Executing A "Beautiful Deleveraging"." https://businessinsider.com/ray-dalio-america-beautiful-deleveraging-2012-5#:~:text=A%20beautiful%20deleveraging%20 balances%20the%20three%20options.%20In,produce%20too%20much-h%20deflation%20or%20too%20much%20depression (accessed November 16, 2020).

DeFi Rate. n.d. *DeFi Job Board*. (https://defirate.com/jobs/). (accessed November 11, 2020).

Fuller, T. 2020. WikiQuote. https://en.wikiquote.org/wiki/Thomas_Fuller_ (writer) (accessed November 9, 2020).

Glassdoor Team. January 10, 2020. Glassdoor. *15 More Companies That No Longer Require a Degree—Apply Now*, https://glassdoor.com/blog/no-degree-required/ (accessed November 15, 2020).

Gretchen, M., and G. Emily. April 26, 2018. "The Wall Street Journal." *Wells Fargo's 401(k) Practices Probed by Labor Department*. (accessed November 10, 2020).

Jenkins, R. Inc. July 2017. "Generation Z Versus Millennials: The 8 Differences You Need to Know." https://inc.com/ryan-jenkins/generation-z-vs-millennials-the-8-differences-you-.html (accessed November 14, 2020).

Julian. 2020. "How Much Money Yes Theory Makes On YouTube – Net Worth." https://naibuzz.com/much-money-yes-theory-makes-youtube-net-worth-2/ (accessed November 6, 2020).

Kikaon, T. September 2018. "Affinity." *Yes Theory Is Changing the World and Here's Why*. http://culture.affinitymagazine.us/yes-theory-is-changing-the-world-and-heres-why/ (accessed November 8, 2020)

Maida, J. November 4, 2020. "Businesswire." *Global Food Delivery Services Market to Reach USD 215.56 Billion by 2024, Stimulated by Growing Mergers and Acquisitions*. https://businesswire.com/news/home/20201104005424/en/ (accessed November 8, 2020).

Nandi, S. 2020. "Digital Journal." *HYVE – Catering to the Demands of the Fast Growing Gig Economy Using Power of Decentralization*, http://digitaljournal.com/pr/4869589 (accessed November 9, 2020).

November 2020. "Board of Governors of the Federal Reserve System." *Consumer Credit - G.19*. https://federalreserve.gov/releases/g19/current/ (accessed November 16, 2020).

O'Dell, C. 2020. "Parks Perspectives." *Smart Home Opportunities for Home Builders*. http://parksassociates.com/blog/article/smart-home-opportunities-for-home-builders (accessed November 11, 2020).

Portero, A. December 9, 2011. "International Business Times." *30 Major U.S. Corporations Paid More to Lobby Congress Than Income Taxes*, 2008–2010. (accessed November 10, 2020).

Rigby, S. 2020. "Science Focus." *5G: Driverless Cars Could Warn Each Other of Dangers Using New Network*. https://sciencefocus.com/news/5g-driverless-cars-could-warn-each-other-of-dangers-using-new-network/ (accessed November 11, 2020).

Sabin, S. 2020. "Morning Consult." *As of May, 5G Workforce Has Added 106,000 Jobs in the U.S., Report Finds.* https://morningconsult.com/2020/09/17/5g-network-jobs-data-report/ (accessed November 11, 2020).

September 2020. "Seeking Alpha." *The Real Problem Behind The $26.8 Trillion U.S. National Debt.* https://seekingalpha.com/article/4374160-real-problem-behind-26_8-trillion-u-s-national-debt (accessed November 16, 2020).

Simon, J.I. 2019. "TechSmith." *Video Statistics, Habits, and Trends You Need To Know [New Research].* https://techsmith.com/blog/video-statistics/ (accessed November 8, 2020).

SWNS. January 30, 2020. New York Post, https://nypost.com/2020/01/30/alarming-number-of-americans-dont-have-enough-savings-for-unexpected-expenses/ (accessed November 15, 2020).

Wikipedia. *Wells Fargo.* https://en.wikipedia.org/wiki/Wells_Fargo (accessed November 10, 2020).

About the Author

Rodd Mann, MBA, CPA, CGMA, CPIM is the CEO/Founder of Rodd Mann Consulting in Irvine, CA, a finance project consulting firm. He has served in a variety of top accounting, finance, manufacturing operations, and consulting roles in large, global high-tech companies. He has worked in manufacturing cost accounting, held the positions of Corporate Controller and Vice President of Finance, as well as run materials, logistics and was the Vice President of Manufacturing Operations in global high-tech multi-billion-dollar firms.

He worked at Texas Instruments, Western Digital, Seagate, Kingston Technology, and several tech firms. He traveled extensively throughout the world his entire career, managing large, complex financial and operational issues in this fast-changing tech world.

Besides his BBA and MBA, along with certifications such as CPA (Certified Public Accountant), AICPA's CGMA (Chartered Global Management Accountant), and APIC's CPIM (American Production and Inventory Control—Certification in Production and Inventory Management), he has completed coursework in two doctoral programs, Doctor of Business Administration (DBA) and Doctor of Education (EdD).

Rodd Mann has made presentations on financial metrics, modeling, and critical analysis for the IOFM (Institute of Financial Managers), CFO Roundtable, and FEI (Financial Executives Institute).

He was also Adjunct Professor of Finance, at Concordia University, in Irvine, CA for 4 years where he both taught and developed an online version of his Finance course.

Index

OTHER TITLES IN THE ENTREPRENEURSHIP AND SMALL BUSINESS MANAGEMENT COLLECTION

Scott Shane, Case Western University, Editor

- *Native American Entrepreneurs* by Ron P. Sheffield and Mark J. Munoz
- *Blockchain Value* by Olga V. Mack
- *TAP Into Your Potential* by Rick De La Guardia
- *Stop, Change, Grow* by Michael Carter and Karl Shaikh
- *From Starting Small to Winning Big* by Shishir Mishra
- *Dynastic Planning* by Walid S. Chiniara
- *How to Succeed as a Solo Consultant* by Stephen D. Field
- *Small Business Management* by Andreas Karaoulanis
- *Department of Startup* by Ivan Yong Wei Kit and Sam Lee
- *The Entrepreneurial Adventure* by David James and Oliver James
- *Cultivating an Entrepreneurial Mindset* by Tamiko L. Cuellar
- *On All Cylinders, Second Edition* by Ron Robinson
- *From Vision to Decision* by Dana K. Dwyer
- *Get on Board* by Olga V. Mack
- *The Rainmaker* by Jacques Magliolo
- *Family Business Governance* by Keanon J. Alderson

Announcing the Business Expert Press Digital Library

Concise e-books business students need for classroom and research

This book can also be purchased in an e-book collection by your library as

- a one-time purchase,
- that is owned forever,
- allows for simultaneous readers,
- has no restrictions on printing, and
- can be downloaded as PDFs from within the library community.

Our digital library collections are a great solution to beat the rising cost of textbooks. E-books can be loaded into their course management systems or onto students' e-book readers.
The **Business Expert Press** digital libraries are very affordable, with no obligation to buy in future years. For more information, please visit **www.businessexpertpress.com/librarians**. To set up a trial in the United States, please email **sales@businessexpertpress.com**.

www.ingramcontent.com/pod-product-compliance
Lightning Source LLC
Chambersburg PA
CBHW061334220326
41599CB00026B/5180